Heidi Goehmann writes with such clarity [and] brokenness in our tangle of experiences [and] points us to hope. Personally engaging, theologically honesty and grace, this book will give you joy in the midst of the struggle. A great read I can't wait to share with my friends!

Rev. Dr. Justin Rossow, author and founder of Next Step Press

Heidi's words of truth and grace meet the reader with gentleness and compassion as she graciously brings our eyes to see the beauty of hope. This book reminds us that although life is messy and heavy and painful, hope is real. And hope is for us. Hope meets our brokenness and leads our eyes above, fixing them on the One who loves us. As you lose yourself in Heidi's words, she will guide you forward to see how Christ brings restoration through His overwhelming love and grace.

Tanner Olson, author, poet, and speaker, Writtentospeak.com

Goehmann speaks truth to the experience of living in a broken world—life is hard. Instead of piling on the false hope of self-improvement, Goehmann consistently points readers to Christ's unrelenting grace and mercy. The world needs the hope that this book brings—not hope in our earthy rulers, relationships, or job status, but hope in the restorative Gospel of Christ Jesus.

Bethany Werner, director of Children
and Family Ministries, Messiah Lutheran Church

Brokenness. Pain. Deep disappointment. Heidi Goehmann addresses life's dark moments with candor, honesty, and, above all, hope—Christian hope. She candidly shows us our own sin and how it impacts our family, community, and God's creation. The book is saturated with Scripture and always leads to Jesus. Heidi's key text is Romans 5:5, "Hope does not disappoint"—and, I would add, neither will her book.

Rev. Dr. Reed Lessing, professor of theology and ministry
and director of the Center for Biblical Studies, Concordia University, St. Paul

Brokenness is a covert enemy. It eats away at our sense of purpose and teaches despair and doubt. In *Finding Hope: From Brokenness to Restoration*, Heidi shows us God's response to brokenness. Instead of leaving us to deny it or dwell on it, He uses brokenness as a step stool to the sure hope of Jesus Christ. Hope is the answer, and this book shows the way.

Kim Marxhausen, PhD, author

Finding Hope is a must read for anyone curious about the lifelong journey of brokenness toward wholeness. Heidi Goehmann takes readers on an honest and deep quest of understanding and living into the messy paradox of brokenness and hope. Read this book and be affirmed that God's grace touches each part of your life.

Vanessa M. Seifert, PhD, Seifert Leadership Consulting,
and DCE, Calvary Lutheran Church

Christians are used to blaming sin for the troubles they encounter in life. Rightly so. In *Finding Hope*, Heidi Goehmann brings depth and nuance to the sin-problem conversation and gives "a name for the interaction of the messy alongside the good of life." Her assessment of brokenness meets us all and points us toward God and the promise of hope in Jesus. This book is for anyone ready for a meaningful glimpse into their own struggle in this broken creation and offers help to those who want to deal with it head-on.

Katie Nafzger, women's coordinator,
Concordia Seminary, St. Louis

In *Finding Hope*, Heidi Goehmann takes the reader on a unique journey of hope, one found in the ruins of our hurting world. By calling out our brokenness, Goehmann deftly points the reader back to the hope found in Christ and wonderfully explores it in a tangible way to the reader. *Finding Hope* is a must read for those who have been broken by our world and desire something more.

Rev. Ryan Oakes, Gethsemane Lutheran Church

I am happy to recommend *Finding Hope*. Heidi's definitions of terms such as *identity*, *resilience*, and *brokenness* are particularly profound, thought-provoking, and anchored in truth. Heidi has a beautiful way of facing into the hard and leading to Jesus. I look forward to sharing this book with others!

Susan Steege, director of Transformation Ministries,
First Trinity Lutheran Church

Finding Hope is deeply theological while remaining utterly practical. As a mental health professional, Heidi Goehmann does not discount how difficult life in the brokenness can be. As a theologian, she understands the answer to these problems is as simple as Jesus. This book will strike a chord of empathy in your brokenness and at the same time give you deeply theological and utterly practical hope for your yesterday, today, and forever.

Katie Koplin, writer and speaker

finding

FROM BROKENNESS TO RESTORATION

hope

**HEIDI
GOEHMANN**

CONCORDIA PUBLISHING HOUSE · SAINT LOUIS

Published by Concordia Publishing House
3558 S. Jefferson Avenue, St. Louis, MO 63118-3968
1-800-325-3040 • cph.org

Unless otherwise noted, Scripture quotations are from the ESV® Bible (The Holy Bible, English Standard Version®), copyright © 2001 by Crossway, a publishing ministry of Good News Publishers. Used by permission. All rights reserved.

Scripture quotations marked NASB are taken from the New American Standard Bible®, copyright © 1960, 1962, 1963, 1968, 1971, 1972, 1973, 1975, 1977, 1995 by The Lockman Foundation. Used by permission. (www.Lockman.org)

Scripture quotations marked NLT are taken from the Holy Bible, New Living Translation, copyright © 1996, 2004, 2015 by Tyndale House Publishers, a division of Tyndale House Ministries, Carol Stream, Illinois 60188. All rights reserved.

Scripture quotations marked NIV are taken from the Holy Bible, New International Version®. NIV®. Copyright © 1973, 1978, 1984 by Biblica, Inc.™ Used by permission of Zondervan. All rights reserved.

Manufactured in the United States of America

Library of Congress Cataloging-in-Publication Data

Names: Goehmann, Heidi, author.

Title: Finding hope : from brokenness to restoration / Heidi Goehmann.

Description: Saint Louis, MO : Concordia Publishing House, [2021] | Summary: "This book is for anyone who struggles with the messes of life. Each of the four sections addresses a different place where we encounter life's messes: in ourselves, in our family, in our connections with one another, and in the world, all based on the author's experience with friends, acquaintances, and therapy clients. This book is designed to shift the reader's internal focuses; instead of embracing or ignoring the mess, we can find refuge in God as we walk through the mess, confident in His power and control. We can clearly see how God is working in the ugly stuff of life, making it something redeemed and filled with bright and shining hope through Christ"-- Provided by publisher.

Identifiers: LCCN 2020044204 (print) | LCCN 2020044205 (ebook) | ISBN 9780758669346 (paperback) | ISBN 9780758669353 (ebook)

Subjects: LCSH: Hope--Religious aspects--Christianity. | Trust in God--Christianity. | Healing--Religious aspects--Christianity.

Classification: LCC BV4638 .G64 2021 (print) | LCC BV4638 (ebook) | DDC 234/.25--dc23

LC record available at https://lccn.loc.gov/2020044204

LC ebook record available at https://lccn.loc.gov/2020044205

1 2 3 4 5 6 7 8 9 10   30 29 28 27 26 25 24 23 22 21

To my mom,
who knew the
shadows of
brokenness and held
tenaciously to Hope

Contents

WHAT IS BROKENNESS?

Last year I turned forty years old. I celebrated my birthday with much pomp and circumstance. My friends carried me off for a day of deliciously dark coffee, thrift store treasures, Mexican food, a Ferris wheel, a concert, and more love than any human can realistically expect during the course of a single calendar day. They reminded me life is worth celebrating.

That summer our family took a long-planned, long-saved-for, long-awaited camping trip that put 4,718 miles on our minivan. We hiked, we argued about which song to play or audiobook to listen to during the hours and hours of driving, we sat by campfires and discussed life and God, we got eaten alive by black flies, and we passed food around tables while also passing love and affection to one another.

Then we came home. We unpacked and did laundry. We ate breakfasts and dinners around our hundred-year-old family table. I wrote articles for my website and put out videos about mental health. My husband, Dave, preached sermons and led movie nights for college students. A new school year started, and the kids went back to school. Our two youngest kids learned some new math and read all the books they could devour. Our teenagers started high school for their first and their final years. We talked about putting our ice rink in the front yard instead of the back yard. We went for walks, and I bought groceries. Life was so normal I could taste it, and it tasted good, like a big Sunday dinner full of comfort and love and nourishment.

Yet, there was something else. For me, everything also began to feel weighty and sluggish, like I had put on pajamas and couldn't take them off. When I sat still in the evening before bed, I noticed there was more than tiredness in my bones. I was sad. I was a little bit angry, mildly put off by life and its very existence.

My husband turned to me one night and said, "So . . ." in a drawn-out way that allowed my tears to finally come. There was no concrete reason for their presence. I was a woman full of privilege. I had a home and food and new tennis shoes. My kids were thriving. I had just gotten back from visiting a friend in Germany. My husband would never accuse, but the voice of my conscience had plenty of accusation to spare: "What is your problem, Heidi? Get it together."

I knew I needed some help.

I called in my six free sessions with a counselor through my husband's employer. I scrolled through name after name of therapists on the list. I looked at their pictures on their websites and read about their specialties. I called the one who seemed knowledgeable but also had an open, friendly smile. I showed up for my appointment and sat down on her couch, where the words started tumbling out: "I don't get it. I'm fine. We're fine. Everything is fine. It's all so very fine I could scream for the fine-ness of it."

My therapist asked slow-paced questions, listened intently to my many, many words, handed me tissues, and told me this wisdom: "Some things are worthy of grief, even when we cannot see them."

She was right. While my days were spinning along "just fine," the current season had also made me suddenly aware of life's perpetual forward motion. Alongside all the goodness in my life— daily adventures with my family, friendships that filled me with affection, a sense of purpose in my work—sat some other stuff. My mom was getting older and had some significant health concerns. My oldest daughter was visiting colleges, submitting for scholarships and grants, crying under the pressure, and making choices for the next leg of her journey. I had just released a book I felt passionate about, but which also had left behind significant cognitive and emotional residue.

As I lingered with my thoughts after each therapy session, I realized I needed a name for the interaction of the messy alongside the good of life. I needed to understand more about the turmoil, the stress, the gunk, and the blahs that can be so persistently present in life, even when each day brings so much beauty and blessing.

When I probed deeper and searched wider, the concept of brokenness fit the bill.

Brokenness is weighty. It holds sadness but isn't far removed from joy. It's abstract and experienced differently by each of us, but also universal and experienced by everyone. It is a neighbor who has always lived next door, but whom we maybe haven't happened to meet. Most of us have likely not walked up to brokenness to ask its name or find out its backstory. Brokenness is always there though, ever present, a continual reminder that life is hard and worthwhile and never quite what we thought it was going to be.

Still, I have *known* brokenness. You have known brokenness. We have spent time with brokenness. We are all sinners, saved only by grace. We might each know on a theological or cognitive level that the world was and is impacted by the brokenness of sin. However, I hadn't really allowed God to tend to the truth of what brokenness is beyond that level. The concept of brokenness wasn't a part of my daily life and my language cache. Until I felt its weight pressing in, I hadn't taken the time to evaluate and reflect on the impact of brokenness for me, for my family, or for my neighbor.

Yet brokenness will not be ignored. It makes its presence known at some point. Families are messy, mine included. I create messes wherever I go with sharp words and things left undone. God and I meet often to talk about my issues and my wrecks. Brokenness also comes in the form of other people's wrecks and issues. We have all likely suffered at the hands of someone else's sharp words and those things they have left undone. Relationships require vulnerability, but also boundaries in this life. Forgiveness is indispensable, but that doesn't make it easy.

Some of the brokenness we encounter we can overtly label as the sin inside each of us—our thoughts, our desires, our actions. Some of the brokenness we encounter is clearly the sin inside our neighbor—their thoughts, their desires, their behaviors. However, brokenness also comes more abstractly in the form of unemployment, children lost too soon, or mental health struggles busting through our back door in the middle of the night like a burglar. Brokenness is a wider concept that encompasses the complete mess brought into the world when sin first arrived on the scene.

To put it more simply, brokenness is our experience of sin in this life in four realms.

To put it more simply, brokenness is our experience of sin in this life in four realms. We each experience the impact of sin in every one of these realms, most likely every day.

1. My own sin, my messy sin, all my messy sin.

2. The sin of others, as well as the messy mistakes and hurt their sin brings into our lives.

3. That which we call *original sin*—the very first sin brought into the world in Genesis 3 that changed the fabric of our DNA, as well as the fabric of the oceans and land and all the natural processes within them. Original sin impacts the fabric of the entire universe in all its breadth and depth; it is the consequence of that first fall on all people and all things.

4. And finally, the broadest brokenness—our internal *awareness* of the cracks in the whole structure. An awareness of all that is broken inside of us and around us is also a consequence of that first fall. We can categorize this awareness under original sin, but I think it serves us well to acknowledge it separately too. There is a *heaviness* to life, a weight, that wasn't there before sin came in. It reminds us that it wasn't supposed to be this way and whispers inside each of us, "There must be something more."

Each and every one of us will find the weight of brokenness pressing into our lives at different times, in our moments of contemplation, sometimes in our moments of victory, but especially in our moments of despair. Brokenness is both our internal experience of shame and hurt and pain and our relational experience of those things. Brokenness is the reality of living on a planet that is slowly dying, which we steward to the best of our abilities, but which will also bear the brunt of sin's existence alongside us. Like the atmosphere surrounding planet Earth, brokenness also covers the fallen world. It turns in revolution with the earth and all the stars. It changes the air we breathe.

But so does Christ. His restoration covers all and is in all.

When Christ died on the cross, He took on every sin and also every shame. He held the weight of brokenness in His chest and cried its anthem with, "My God, My God, why have You forsaken Me?" (Matthew 27:46; Mark 15:34). Christian believers can be assured that the weight of brokenness is no longer theirs to bear; Christ covers all our brokenness in His redemption. Yet we live in a now-and-not-yet world. While all brokenness has been redeemed on the cross, there remains this time we live in when we wait for all brokenness to be restored. We will still feel brokenness pressing in, and we will bear some parts of brokenness in our lives until we see the Bearer of every shame face-to-face. In Christ Jesus, we live in the knowledge that there is something better to come, that sorrow and hurt last for the night, but joy will come—joy does come—in the morning (Psalm 30:5). What we see in front of us won't be broken for all eternity.

This awareness of brokenness brings struggle and wrestling into our lives. God will certainly use this wrestling for His good, but it won't be removed until Christ comes again. The force of the wrestling feels all too reminiscent of the weight of our sin. Satan will use this constantly to his advantage. He wants our awareness of brokenness to weigh us down in the shame that was lifted from us on the cross long ago. When we don't talk about the concept of brokenness or understand its impact on our lives, we can end up applying shame to ourselves and to others around us who are asking for help in this broken world. Brokenness isn't always about what we individually have done wrong, although that's part of it. Brokenness also isn't always about what we as humanity do wrong. Sometimes it simply means that we reside in a sinful world and we are all people impacted by sin in every area of our life.

When we do not have language for the things of this world that are broken, we end up with very few ways to confess these things before God. We can easily end up believing there is something wrong with us: "What's wrong with me that I lost my house in the tornado when my neighbor didn't?" Or we can end up blaming those around us: "Well, if they would just have done x, y, and z, they could have avoided losing their house in that tornado."

These are both examples of shame. Shame is the belief that something is inherently *so* wrong with us that we are not able to receive God's grace. It obscures our view of both Jesus' sacrifice and love for us. Because shame is naturally isolating, we can also be tempted to throw it onto others in the form of blame; it's weirdly more comforting to be in a club of shame than riding that train on our own. I believe that calling brokenness by name helps us to more accurately apply guilt and accountability where it belongs in our lives and the lives of those we love. It also helps us acknowledge the impact of brokenness on our lives without allowing the devil to stack weights of unproductive shame that beat us down from the inside. Acknowledged guilt, coupled with God's Word, turns us to Christ. Shame turns us into ourselves and away from Christ. With Jesus in our lives, shame has no place. Calling brokenness by name allows us to properly see the place of the Law, to acknowledge it even, so that we can walk through it to get to the sweetness of the Gospel.

Brokenness disrupts the good things of this life almost every time. Many of us stand grateful to God for all we've been given so graciously. We don't want to disrupt that gratefulness. We can try to ignore the mess and chaos for a little while in favor of all the good in life; that way we don't have to deal with the grief and fear that brokenness brings. Or we can try to aggressively wield control over our lives, attempting to annihilate the mess all on our own. But neither of those responses are sustainable mentally or emotionally. Brokenness will eventually return, and our house of cards will fall.

Instead of good and only good, God gives us something in the middle of the brokenness. He gives us hope.

The answer really is as simple and as complicated as Jesus. As always, the Savior of our souls is also the Savior of this whole wide world and the universe beyond. He walks into the messy things of life alongside us. He does not forsake us in our darkest hours, nor does He forsake us in our questions and wonderings. His death on the cross and His resurrection brought humankind salvation. The redemption price for God's people is paid. Hallelujah, Christ is risen.

Crucifixion hope, resurrection hope, restoration hope in Jesus lifts the weight of all brokenness from our minds and off of our chests. Hope resides alongside the awareness in our hearts and minds and acts as a life raft, propping us up from underneath. Jesus' hope says to me and to you, "There will be a time when all of this will be made new, when DNA will be made right and every chromosome will be perfectly in place, when famine and poverty will cease and violence will end, when the whole of creation will spring up alive in a new way. And it will be remarkable! This is not all there is. This is a good life, but it is not the best one."

Hope is a wonderful solution that still feels messy to us. We see hope imperfectly now, but one day we will see it perfectly. First Corinthians 13:12 describes it best: "For now we see in a mirror dimly, but then face to face. Now I know in part; then I shall know fully, even as I have been fully known."

While we see and experience imperfectly, be assured God sees all things in perfection. It's wild that even our experience of hope in this life is touched by brokenness. Yet we are undaunted. Hope, biblically, is a confident expectation of all that God is and all that He has planned. There will be times in my life when I have a hard time experiencing things like faith and hope in their fullness, but they are still there, real and true in Christ Jesus. We will see the presence of hope more clearly when we walk into the mess and call it by name: brokenness. We will also likely wrestle with brokenness and hope before God. By definition, hope is best found in the messes and the mistakes of life, the hurts and the struggles, rather than in the victories or in the glory. Hope isn't really hope until you need it.

This hope, Christ's hope, does not disappoint. Romans 5:5 in the New American Standard Bible translation affirms this: "Hope does not disappoint, because the love of God has been poured out within our hearts through the Holy Spirit who was given to us." Hope "does not disappoint" not because people around us do not disappoint, and not because the world does not disappoint, but because Jesus does not disappoint.

Romans 5:5 in the English Standard Version of the Bible gets right to the heart of the matter. God's hope is meant to lift the weight of all the shame that Satan tries to sneak in each day, "And hope does not put us to shame, because God's love has been poured into our hearts through the Holy Spirit who has been given to us."

Hope is poured into us in Jesus' death and resurrection. Jesus wasn't afraid to walk into the mess of humanity. He opened Himself to experiencing all the messes this world had to offer and experiencing them fully. He has known about the mess brokenness would cause since the creation of the world, but He came here anyway and experienced our messes firsthand, as a baby, as a child, and then as a man—thirty-three years in the middle of the mess. He brought hope into our lives by stretching Himself out on an ugly cross. He rose so that we would know His hope is life-giving hope. God the Spirit came into the messy world at Pentecost (Acts 2) and into each of our lives most clearly in our Baptism. His presence is hope in our mess each day, every day. Because we are baptized believers, the Spirit of the living God calls these messy bodies of ours home. Our God does not flee or leave us in our mess. He nestles in closer. When we acknowledge brokenness, the Holy Spirit still enlightens and never stops calling. God doesn't desert us in our brokenness. Jesus never leaves us when we allow ourselves to say, "This is hard." Rather, when we call brokenness by name, we can begin to find hope.

INTRODUCTION

FROM BROKENNESS TO HOPE

hope*

1 a confident expectation of all that God is and all that He has planned

2 truly possible only in the death and resurrection of Jesus Christ, our Savior

3 looking, face forward, to the return of Jesus Christ, our Restorer

4 small things in our lives that remind us there is something better ahead

This book is designed to shift our internal focuses, to move us from white-knuckling the messes of life to recognizing them and naming them, calling them brokenness out loud. By moving through brokenness, we can more clearly see hope and discern

---

* The definitions at the beginning of each segment of this book are my own. I relied on Scripture as well as many books and internet definitions to help me develop them. They have not been field tested with research participants or any other scientific method. They are imperfect but intended to help us grapple with the tension between what God says about these things in His Word, what is revealed to us in the sciences of psychology and sociology, and how we understand them within our cultural contexts.

God's presence in the middle of our daily lives, whether we're experiencing joy or sorrow or both simultaneously.

What in your life begs for an introduction to Hope—to Jesus and His active restoration in our lives?

I find that in opening up the conversation about brokenness and its messes, people need a few upfront acknowledgments in order to create a zone of safe discovery:

- First, the messiness of life can be incredibly uncomfortable.

  Hope says, God is the God of all comfort (2 Corinthians 1:3).

- Second, very little in life has easy answers.

  Hope says, Be encouraged. We have access in Jesus to ask any question before the One who holds all the answers (Hebrews 6:17–20).

- Third, the concepts of brokenness and hope can be very abstract, making hope seem far away at times.

  Hope in Christ says, God makes things clear in His time. This one can be especially hard to believe. Hear the words of Jesus: "Nothing is covered up that will not be revealed, or hidden that will not be known" (Luke 12:2).

- Last, the chaos and lack of clarity in this life often leave us feeling alone. We can feel like we have been left by God to clean up the world all on our own. It can also seem like we are the only people who have struggled in a particular way.

  Hope says, God values our experiences of mess as much as He values our experiences of joy and glory. Grace is active in our lives every day. Grace means that Jesus is with us in the brokenness, working in the brokenness. He does not turn His face from our brokenness (John 1:5, 14).

Our lives are a process, not a product. Our faith is a process, not a product. Brokenness is a part of each and every one of us. Brokenness in the world impacts each and every one of us. I wrote this book to help you identify your unique narrative of brokenness. What messes have you encountered in your life? Where has brokenness pressed in and pushed forward around you? My goal is to help you find hope by first calling brokenness by name. Christ does not leave us in this process. Jesus' presence—through God's Word and the Holy Spirit—helps us recognize the broken parts of life and still honor the beauty of the life we've been given. There is also a world out there full of people who need to know hope, to know that brokenness isn't always cloaked in blame and fault-finding. They need honesty and kindness in helping them name the brokenness that presses into their lives, their families, and their communities. As we identify the brokenness together, we will also help one another see where Jesus touches the broken places and things of our lives. He is never far from each bit of the brokenness we encounter. We can both recognize His presence in the narratives of our lives and ask Him to go deeper into our hearts and minds to reveal more of His presence in our narratives of brokenness. We aren't celebrating or embracing the mess together; we're unveiling it together for His healing.

We aren't celebrating or embracing the mess together; we're unveiling it together for His healing.

There are many, many things we want fixed or solved in this life. More than a solution, though, we desire hope. In this book, in addition to naming brokenness, we will look together for how hope shows up time and again in Jesus Christ. This book will work through some of the broad impacts of brokenness in our lives and world, to help you identify your own experiences of brokenness. We will focus on the areas that come up most often with clients in my therapy practice, with my friends, and in discussions I see online, giving particular attention to how brokenness impacts our identity, our relationships, and our sense of belonging.

Hope is contagious. When the hope of Christ touches one mess, it tends to roll over into another mess and then another. As we find hope in one thing, God will open the window to let the spring air of hope into all kinds of spaces in our lives.

To keep the messes contained and organized, this book is neatly divided into four sections (if you see the irony in that, we'll get along just fine):

Messes in Me: Broken Identity

Messes in Family: Broken Intimacy

Messes in Community: Broken Belonging

Messes in Creation: A Broken World

In each of these areas—self, family, community, and the world at large—we will deal with obvious messes and less obvious ones. We will encounter both internal and external chaos. We will verbalize the struggle, which is a powerful thing. And we will find out what God has to say about these manifestations of brokenness and those things touched by brokenness in our lives.

We will find hope in the promises of restoration God has given us and see the hope Jesus brings into our lives each day.

For instance, I have messes *in me*. You have messes *in you*. Brokenness is at work when we get the flu bug, battle things like cancer or diabetes, or figure out we hate the taste of kale even though it's good for us. But what messes are found in these bodies that are harder to see on the surface? Messes like body image, mental health challenges, and chronic pain are not uncommon. Many of us, at one time or another, have battled an internal monologue of shame and criticism. We might feel like we have control of our thoughts and emotions in one moment and our thoughts and emotions have control of us in the next. These examples of brokenness inside of us have a great impact on how we see ourselves and our relationships, as well as how we see God at work in our lives.

We also each have messes in our families. The touch of brokenness on our families feels intimate and personal. We look around and wonder whether we are the only ones struggling with family dynamics. We don't want to confront the hard parts of our childhood or the things that thwart our sense of safety, of a snug, thriving family. Basic life decisions about marrying, moving, taking jobs, or having kids can feel messy. There are expectations all around us about how our family should communicate and connect. Families are complicated and have many layers, which makes us want to tuck the conversation away for another day. What if we talked about these complications and honored them for a moment together?

Relationships with friends, a support system outside of our family, are also important. Yet isolation is real. Disconnection and loneliness can be found all around us and sometimes within us. Brokenness impacts our sense of community and our sense of belonging. Brokenness makes strong boundaries necessary in some relationships. It makes words and actions hard to discern. And brokenness is felt maybe worst with the sting of rejection. Even the Body of Christ, designed by God Himself, can be complicated and messy. Unfortunately, brokenness is found even in the Church because it involves broken people living in a broken world.

The brokenness of the world is evident when we hear about natural disasters on the news or experience the evil and hurt one human can cause another. From online conversations to plate tectonics, brokenness leaves cracks wherever it surfaces. *All* of creation cries out, groaning to God for help, just as we do. Every blade of grass, every star in the sky, every government, every strand of DNA is impacted by the fruit that was supposed to remain on a tree in the Garden of Eden. We experience mental health struggles, trauma, and loss upon loss. In looking closer at the ripples of brokenness in the whole world, we also find the wide circles of hope that Jesus draws around every area of our lives and every corner of our universe.

I have noticed that we are often scared to name brokenness, to become more aware of it, to call it out and name it because we wonder if we recognize it, and especially if we call it by name, it might stick around. We worry it might stir up more brokenness, like dust bunnies filling a room, wildfire smoke filling the air we breathe. When brokenness leans into our lives and gets close, we want to push it away. We don't want brokenness to think it can hang out any longer than it already has. We don't want brokenness to settle in for an overnight stay. We are terrified that brokenness might leave a stain we can't soak or scrub away. But I have also noticed that healing and hope come *through* the brokenness, not around it. Long ago, Jesus walked through the brokenness of this world, taking our sin and brokenness to the cross to bring us healing. That looked foolish to the world around Him, and our walk into brokenness rather than around it might look foolish to the world around us. But the brokenness of the cross is itself the power of God:

> For the word of the cross is folly to those who are perishing, but to us who are being saved it is the power of God. . . . For Jews demand signs and Greeks seek wisdom, but we preach Christ crucified, a stumbling block to Jews and folly to Gentiles, but to those who are called, both Jews and Greeks, Christ the power of God and the wisdom of God. For the foolishness of God is wiser than men, and the weakness of God is stronger than men. (1 Corinthians 1:18, 22–25)

As much as we'd like to and no matter how hard we try, we can't bypass brokenness. Let me assure you, Christ remains in control in all the brokenness, in all *our* brokenness. Brokenness is still under His throne. And because it happens under His throne, brokenness is never outside of His hope.

In this book, we'll work toward seeing His hope more clearly. Together we will look life's messes in the eye and call them by name:

"I see you, brokenness. No more hiding."

In this book, we will walk together to find hope.

MESSES IN ME:
BROKEN IDENTITY

identity

1 a sense of who we are as a person

2 a sense of who we are in Christ Jesus

It's always a good practice to take a moment occasionally and reflect on where we've been and where we're going in this life. When we see God's faithfulness in where He has brought us, we can actively apply and expect that faithfulness where we are today and where we'll be tomorrow. Some of our reflections will be serious; others may be humorous. Frequently, we might find ourselves with a mix of both. God seems to work that way. Life, and God's work in it, is anything but simple. It is encouraging to know that while we might wrestle with concepts and ideas about God and life, God's character remains the same always. And all we truly need to know of God is that Jesus died and rose for every one of us.

When I reflect on brokenness God has brought me through, I think of myself laid out on a gurney in an emergency room in Ohio, listening to a medical diagnosis that sounded a little more like a daytime talk show than I preferred. The first doctor I saw declared he had no idea what was wrong with me, and then said nonchalantly, "Your symptoms kind of remind me of this thing I read about in a John Grisham novel once called dengue fever."

Nothing incites confidence quite like a John Grisham diagnosis. It took four ER visits, three hospitals, and ten days with a team of doctors from infectious disease, neurology, and internal medicine to diagnose me with . . . yep, dengue fever.

Dengue fever is miserable. It's tempting to use comparative suffering when we are confronted with misery. Comparative suffering is that game we play where we begin listing the things that are "worse" than our sorrows and sufferings of the moment. We think this will make us feel better, or make a friend who is struggling feel better, but it rarely does. When someone is suffering, it hurts. Comparative suffering offers positivity, but what we really need is hope. Hope is the voice of Christ saying, "I see you," to Hagar in her miserable moment (Genesis 21:15–21), rather than the voice of Christ saying, "Look at all this other misery around you."

Comparative suffering offers positivity, but what we really need is hope. Hope is the voice of Christ saying, "I see you."

Often, we don't see the full story of someone's suffering anyway. When I was diagnosed with dengue fever, my family had just made the difficult decision to evacuate from our mission and social work experience in Haiti because of concerns regarding one of our children's health. It took us a long time to recover from the illness and heartache of that year. Sure, I could say, "Well, it wasn't cancer"—and that would be a glorious truth—but that wouldn't take away the sense of brokenness sitting on my chest. It wasn't only the physical illness of dengue that struck me hard and fast; it was the brokenness of spirit that comes with the awareness of the brokenness of our bodies. When I looked at disease and disappointment in my life, I felt the identities I had built for myself unravel—healthy, strong, able, missionary, changemaker, adventurer. The yuck and the sadness of that season entered my life like an unwelcome guest and left me asking God, "Who am I? Because if I am Yours, then why all of this?"

When we are confronted with a strange tropical disease, pneumonia, cancer, dementia, or any number of illnesses that assail the body, we are also confronted with a surprising realization: We are not completely in control of these vessels made of skin and bones. Our bodies don't always obey our commands and fulfill our desires. They are mortal, needy, and sometimes rather untrustworthy. Our bodies fall apart, and they fall apart in many, many ways. In this life in the body, we confront other things that disappoint as well—emotional turbulence, career decisions, sexual desires that can be hard to keep in check. All of these things leave us with questions about who we are and what makes up who we are. Our identity is the concept of who we are as people. It is a collision of our muscles and our minds, our hearts, our personalities, our spirits. Hope is found in an identity firmly planted in Christ alone. But that identity, like everything else, is impacted by what we call brokenness.

BROKENNESS
AND DISINTEGRATION

brokenness

1 the existence and awareness of sin and all that is broken in us and around us

2 the state of being separated into two or more pieces

3 the quality of being fractured, splintered, torn, cracked, ruptured, confused, crushed, disorganized, and/or disintegrated

disintegration

1 the *process* of breaking down

2 the loss in integrity of a structure, the loss of solidity, or the introduction of decay

By nature, we want things to fit and work together. We want all the parts in a project to conform neatly and to do their jobs. We want the gears of life to turn continuously without interruption.

Brokenness disrupts the vision of harmony we desire. In a world driven by ideals of peace, satisfaction, and tranquility, even saying the word *broken* aloud can feel like inviting disaster over for dinner. One of the reasons we don't talk about hard things is because, deep inside of us, we wonder whether the whole machine of life would just stop working entirely if these things were said aloud and given a space. We worry we'll have to put up an out-of-order sign on life itself.

The concept of brokenness is complicated and can be a challenge to define neatly. Brokenness is always in our lives, but we notice it at certain times more than others. We will sit down to try and help a friend confront its impact on his or her life, but it's nearly impossible without language to talk about what we're experiencing.

It helps to begin where brokenness began. At one time, there was a garden called Eden and a moment forever branded as "the fall." God created our bodies, as well as everything around us. These miraculous skins of humanity we reside in were at one time untouched by sin. We don't know how long this time of perfection lasted, but its appearance is brief in Scripture, taking up only the first two chapters of Genesis. Then brokenness entered the world in this fall into sin, in Genesis 3. Brokenness touches each of us and everything around us. Brokenness brings suffering, disease, and heartache. Brokenness brings disintegration and deterioration to every fiber of our being and every space that exists in this universe.

Disintegration means the cohesion that once existed in the universe and within our own bodies is no longer. I picture the moment when humans welcomed in sin like a guilty preschooler dropping a vase they were instructed not to touch. I can see Adam and Eve's curiosity welling up, like my own. Without thinking, the vase was changed forever. The perfection of creation was left lying shattered at the feet of our Creator. The rippling impact of this fall might seem unfair, that the whole universe should suffer and hold the blame for the mistake of the first man and woman. But had it not been Adam and Eve, it would have been you and me. Can we see our own capabilities? Sin and the mess of it came into our world and our lives with these first people. Brokenness came with the very first family and entered the very first human relationships. The universe was changed by the hands of those very first keepers of the earth. We would have done the same harm. Humanity is nothing if not capable of mess.

We are all, every one of us, capable of shattering everything. We can hear and affirm our capability of doing much harm because we were created by a God who embodies love and justice, who values both truth and mercy. God knew—He *knew* we would break ourselves, our people, our earth, our present, our future. We can acknowledge the truth of brokenness in us and around us without shame, because this is also true: God loves us enough to create us and to provide the solution to all our messes, mischief, and heartache. God sees us as a parent would see the preschooler standing above the shattered vase. He sees that we are capable of creating trouble and that we are in need of discipline, but He never withholds love. Brokenness doesn't change God's desire to wrap His arms around us. We have a God who loves us enough to send a healer, a Savior, a solution. We have a God who sends Hope.

Jesus heals both our overt sins and the messes the entrance of brokenness brought into the world. In relationship with Jesus, we find healing for our brokenness. His entrance into the world brought hope, and His death on the cross and the empty tomb on Easter morning seal that hope for humanity. The hope of Jesus, then, helps us begin to understand the healing God desires to one day bring to all of creation—every heart, every brain, every plant, every planet.

Until that day of restoration when Christ returns, brokenness impacts the whole universe and brokenness impacts all of us, as well as all parts of us. The consequence of the fall of Genesis 3 is *disintegration*. This overlaps with the concept of entropy in physics and the natural sciences. One of the results of this disintegration is that, internally, we each live with a fragmented sense of self. We struggle to understand ourselves as much as we struggle to understand one another. Wanting things to make sense, we tend toward compartmentalizing ourselves—church Heidi, work Heidi, family-life Heidi. While developmental psychologists often place the work of determining our identity as mostly during our adolescent and teen years, I think the fall into sin means we will do this work throughout our lives.

Our hope lies in God's active, integrating work within us through the person and work of Jesus Christ. True hope begins with a relationship with Jesus. In Jesus Christ, God sees us as fully integrated people. He still sees all the work we need. He sees all our sin. He sees all the brokenness in the world and the unique brokenness found in our own narrative. He is constantly knitting and integrating us back together in His grace and love. We run to the waters of Baptism because we desire to live in this ongoing relationship with God, touched by Christ's hope unquestionably each day.

Any renewal of life, any rebirth, happens by Christ's hand. There are aspects of God's great hope that we can see alive and well in the world all around us, in the same way we can see brokenness in the whole world. God gives us mini messages of hope that point to His goodness and grace: fall turns into winter, which turns into spring; stars die while new ones are born. These things may seem far apart from Christ, but they remind us of the great restoration plan that began before time and hinges on Christ's sacrifice on the cross. One day, all will be made new, all will be fully integrated once again.

We also see hope as God works on the disintegration within us. Our bodies start off broken in this life and end up broken with our deaths. No body works perfectly, even in the tiniest and freshest little ones among us. Our bodies manage to experience brokenness again and again as we go along in this life.

However, through the lens of Christ and His work, God sees us as whole people where we tend to see ourselves only in parts—a messed-up body, a soul that seems lost, or a heart that bursts with joy one day and breaks the next. When we open ourselves up to seeing and naming brokenness in ourselves and in our lives, we will be confronted with our disintegration, but God will also walk beside us to reveal His integration in us and in our lives. Jesus Christ helps us hold brokenness and hope together, rather than bearing the weight of brokenness on our own backs. Like a kaleidoscope, what once looked only like shattered pieces of glass begins to show itself as alive with color, planned and pieced by God as a mosaic.

Scripture specifically reminds us that our bodies are complex and woven miraculously, knit together with impossibly tiny molecules, DNA strands, invisible emotions, miles of capillaries, neural pathways, and much more:

For You formed my inward parts;
    You knitted me together in my mother's womb.
I praise You, for I am fearfully and wonderfully made.
Wonderful are Your works;

my soul knows it very well.
My frame was not hidden from You,
when I was being made in secret,
    intricately woven in the depths of the earth.
Your eyes saw my unformed substance;
in Your book were written, every one of them,
    the days that were formed for me,
    when as yet there was none of them.
    (Psalm 139:13–16)

Even when we believe firmly in God as Creator and knitter, our default vantage point in brokenness is parts and pieces, rather than the greater sense of wholeness God sees. We can find ourselves wrestling with whether God *actually* cares for all our parts as this earthly body starts to fall apart. All it takes is a diagnosis of any physical infirmity—infertility, mental illness, arthritis, dengue fever—for us to find ourselves wrestling with whether God cares about our physical bodies or is really only interested in the salvation of our souls. In Deuteronomy 6:4–7, God reminds His people to concern their whole selves with loving Him and worshiping Him. In sending this reminder, He also assures us that He is invested in every cell in our being—body, heart, soul, and mind:

Hear, O Israel: The LORD our God, the LORD is one.
You shall love the LORD your God with all your heart
and with all your soul and with all your might. And
these words that I command you today shall be on
your heart. You shall teach them diligently to your
children, and shall talk of them when you sit in your
house, and when you walk by the way, and when you
lie down, and when you rise.

When we read these verses, we often focus on what we need to do: talk about God, teach others about God, devote ourselves to God. But God's main message in Scripture is very rarely "Do this" or "Do that." Scripture always points us to Jesus. The entire Bible reveals the brokenness of this world and the incalculable grace of Christ. God is much more concerned in connecting us to Christ and what He's done for us than what we need to be doing beyond that. Scripture is also trinitarian. It shows us Christ in the context of a three-in-one God—Father, Son, and Holy Spirit. God Himself is integration in our disintegrated existence. Therefore, we can only truly understand who we are in relationship to the God who made us. Christ reminds us that He is also concerned with our whole selves when He repeats the words of Deuteronomy in Matthew, Mark, and Luke.

> And He said to him, "You shall love the Lord your God with all your heart and with all your soul and with all your mind. This is the great and first commandment." (Matthew 22:37–38)

> Jesus answered, "The most important is, 'Hear, O Israel: The Lord our God, the Lord is one. And you shall love the Lord your God with all your heart and with all your soul and with all your mind and with all your strength.'" (Mark 12:29–30)

> And He answered, "You shall love the Lord your God with all your heart and with all your soul and with all your strength and with all your mind, and your neighbor as yourself." (Luke 10:27)

Dr. Jeffrey Gibbs, in his commentary on Matthew, reminds the reader not to fixate on the nuances of phrase between the

Deuteronomy passage and each Gospel account. Gibbs notes that these Gospel passages are universally focused on our wholeness. We are whole people—heart, soul, mind, strength—and God is concerned with us and wants to be connected with us entirely, not partially.[1]

In a world without brokenness, we would be fully integrated, we would feel fully integrated, we would look fully integrated—heart, soul, mind, and body. We would be perfectly connected to God. We would perfectly understand ourselves and the world around us. Our bodies would pump blood and send oxygen to all the right places at all the right times without any interruption. Our thyroids would produce the exact amount of each hormone we need, and our brains would send every signal at just the right time across each synapse. After the arrival of brokenness into the world in Genesis 3, that integration is corrupted, like everything else. We end up with bodies that *disintegrate*, quite literally. The curse from Genesis 3 is death, but it didn't look like immediate extinction with the bite into the fruit. Instead, that curse looks like mini deaths over time for the world and each person in it.

This is hope: the curse of brokenness is also a doorway to Jesus Christ.

Our bodies work. They might be cut, but they do heal. Our hearts break, but they mend and strengthen. Our bodies tell us information about what we're feeling, and that may be uncomfortable, but it's also informative. Our minds connect thoughts and words to those feelings and our experiences. And God also gives us His Word. He wrote it down. He prompts us to open it and hear from Him. He connects His Spirit to it and to our whole selves for understanding and for strength. This messy person I call *self* needs attention. God made all of me. He made all of us and loves all our parts and pieces. He sees the brokenness and walks through it with us to create in us a sense of who we are, because we know where we came from and where we're going. We love ourselves, all of ourselves, in our brokenness, because God does. He loved us first, and He'll always love us best.

This is hope: the curse of brokenness is also a doorway to Jesus Christ.

In love, God created a way for His restoration to meet us in our disintegration. His name is Jesus. Because of Jesus' death and resurrection, we have a cord reconnecting us to God. We exist tethered to His integration. The curse of the Law in the brokenness of this life brings daily death; Christ brings daily life. In brokenness, we hold death in our physical bodies; we experience the death of relationships, the death of creativity, the death of dreams. The myriad ways we experience disintegration in this life are meant to point us directly to Hope. The hope of Christ gives us integration now in starts and stops, discoveries and insight, healing and help, but just wait: one day we will receive the full portion of Hope, no roadblocks, no chemo treatments, no miscarriages, no teenage angst, no middle-age unraveling.

In Christ, we find hope.

BODY IMAGE

body image

1 our personal perception and conceptualization of our own physical human body

2 our perception and conceptualization of physical human bodies in general

3 the way we think and feel about our bodies, as well as our behavior toward those bodies

4 the holistic view of one's self as a human being

We are physical beings. As Deuteronomy establishes and the Gospel accounts confirm, God made us body, mind, and spirit. However, Western culture often overvalues physical bodies, and we can get confused, actually undervaluing our physical bodies in an attempt to avoid those cultural values. It's easy to create a mental hierarchy—soul first, maybe mind next, then heart, with the body most likely ending up last. The Bible teaches, rather, that God wants, sees, and values our holistic selves in Christ, not one part over another.

Throughout history, men and women have struggled with body image. Max Factor and Sephora didn't invent makeup; the

Egyptians did, thousands of years ago. Weight, height, mirrors, diet, and exercise aren't all there is to body image. There are also CPAPs and multivitamins, heart murmurs and appendicitis. Body image isn't limited to teenage angst. While we might possibly be aware of our bodies in a unique way in this age of social media, Photoshop, and image filters, all you need to do is visit a natural history museum to see how obsessed the ancients were with presenting and preserving their bodies in just the right way. One of my favorite graphics on the internet is the reminder that Renaissance oil paintings were some of the first selfies. I am inclined to believe that cave paintings may have also been an early contribution. There truly is nothing new under the sun.

Medical definitions of body image tend to be limited to our physical appearance. But body image also includes humankind's struggles with aging and sexuality and health and so much more. We are given a short time on this planet, and we want to get the most out of it. We want to leach as much meaning from this life as we can. We think if we just had a little more time and money and a whole lot more energy, we'd be set. We are massively aware of our positive qualities and also our imperfections. Rather than both being held in tension together, the imperfections often rise quickly to the surface and scream the truth to us that we are limited people, with limited control over this skin we inhabit and our life as a whole.

Psychologists and mental health experts tend to have a wider concept of body image, proposing definitions that reflect the complicated relationship we have with our bodies as more than what we see in the mirror each morning. When you dig into the research surrounding eating disorders, anxiety, and self-esteem struggles, you'll find many resources that encourage us to broaden our definition to include not only what we think and feel about our physical attractiveness but also our reflections, thoughts, feelings, and behaviors surrounding our experience with our physical bodies as a whole. Because of brokenness, we ask questions like, "What makes a person worthy of love?" and "Do I measure up physically?" That brokenness is an important piece of the puzzle in helping us understand why many of us are burdened with body image. These questions and others like them are a reality of the physical dual integration/disintegration present in our bodies until the day Jesus comes back for us. In light of Christ, we can acknowledge the effects of brokenness on our physical selves and in our physical selves. We turn to God's Word and find very real healing for our bodies as well as healing for our view of them.

Our bodies age and walk through a slow decline. Topics such as sexuality and our experiences with our own sexuality can leave us confused and feeling misunderstood. Chronic diseases such as epilepsy, irritable bowel syndrome, or diabetes seem to have missed the memo on hope. We really want cancer to be annihilated and annihilated yesterday. Second Corinthians 4:6–7 likens our bodies to jars of clay:

> For God, who said, "Let light shine out of darkness,"
> has shone in our hearts to give the light of the knowl-
> edge of the glory of God in the face of Jesus Christ.
> But we have this treasure in jars of clay, to show that
> the surpassing power belongs to God and not to us.

Jars of clay are pretty fragile, yet practical. They easily crack or break, but they can almost always be repaired. They might be util-itarian, but they are also blank canvases that can be beautifully decorated. Do we believe that God made our bodies for a purpose, just as He made our souls for a purpose? This passage from 2 Corinthians makes it clear that even these easily shattered, perhaps easily discarded vessels have a purpose. Your body is a vessel God has deemed worthy of salvation and restoration. He valued your body enough to send His Son to die so that it might be redeemed alongside your soul. This physical body is honored enough to be the place intended for His Holy Spirit to reside. In Jesus Christ, God chooses to use you and use your body as a means to give "the light of the knowledge of the glory of God in the face of Jesus Christ" as you walk around this world as a baptized child of God.

There is something different about your spirit when you are baptized. The promise of Baptism is that, in it, God's Spirit takes hold of you and works a mysterious transformation inside of you. As you are baptized, your body becomes an active vessel of hope for other people. The Spirit resides in you, which means Hope resides in you. The mess of the disintegration of our bodies is still there. These earthly bodies are fragile. You age, just like everyone else . . . but not without hope. You might wrestle with your imperfections . . . but not without hope. You might encounter illness . . . but not without hope. Your body might revolt and fail to operate in accordance with the owner's manual. Sometimes you might find yourself sad or angry or frustrated by your own physical challenges and limitations or those that trouble the ones you care about, but you do not face this brokenness without hope.

Our bodies, deeply impacted by the brokenness of the world, also force the question, "Which lives have value?" God is ready and waiting with an answer: "This one," He says. "And this one. And this one. And don't forget about this one over here." When we look at the world around us, we must wrestle with the brokenness of it all—the devaluing and the disparaging and the underestimating. This is not God's hope, and it can be hard to see the hope through the hurt.

It's the brokenness of things, our need for help and answers, that leads us and those around us to hope. Hope isn't hope if we don't need it. We always need Jesus, but we don't always *see* that we need Jesus. When bodies break down, or when the physical things of this world show us their limitations, we become intensely aware of our need.

Hope isn't something we turn to when life is peachy. We often fail to notice hope when we can't see the disintegration up close and personal. Any manifestation of brokenness in physical bodies attacks how we see our physical bodies. But each of those manifestations is also a place where God's hope can shine light into this dark world.

God heals these cracked vessels. He heals them in small ways all the time—cells regenerate, the brain's gray matter deteriorates but also grows, ligaments and muscles lose flexibility but also gain flexibility with exercise and movement. When our bodies simply do what we need them to do, it can be easy to have our own prosperity Gospel-of-the-flesh—"Look at me! God must really love me! I can do all the things!" But when the brokenness comes closer to us, when the deterioration of this disintegrating world becomes more evident in our physical bodies, we stand in a place where God can lift our heads one millimeter to see Hope more clearly.

Second Corinthians continues in the same chapter with this reminder:

So we do not lose heart. Though our outer self is wasting away, our inner self is being renewed day by day. For this light momentary affliction is preparing for us an eternal weight of glory beyond all comparison, as we look not to the things that are seen but to the things that are unseen. For the things that are seen are transient, but the things that are unseen are eternal. (4:16–18)

This is hope: because Jesus has come for you, and is coming for you, there is more to your story than brokenness.

The idea of wasting away sounds weighty to our hearts, our minds, and our souls. When you are the one undergoing a physical trial, the weight of wasting away can add to our exhaustion. We want God to lift our burden from us. And sometimes He does. Many times, though, instead of transforming this physical experience to something perfect today, He simply reminds us that He walks alongside us through it. We feel the weight of aging, of body image, of illness and disease in this life, and that weight brings to mind the weightlessness of the glory to come. First Corinthians 15:42–43 gives us a clearer picture of the weight of glory, which we are awaiting when Christ returns for us. The New Living Translation uses the term *brokenness* in this passage, where other translations more commonly use the term *dishonor*:

It is the same way with the resurrection of the dead. Our earthly bodies are planted in the ground when we die, but they will be raised to live forever. Our bodies are buried in brokenness, but they will be raised in glory. They are buried in weakness, but they will be raised in strength.

This is hope: because Jesus has come for you, and is coming for you, there is more to your story than brokenness. Even with brokenness in us and around us, we live and dance today. We talk and laugh today. God sees the burden of brokenness that we feel. God hears our body's groaning just as He hears our laughter and conversation:

> For we know that if the tent that is our earthly home is destroyed, we have a building from God, a house not made with hands, eternal in the heavens. For in this tent we groan, longing to put on our heavenly dwelling, if indeed by putting it on we may not be found naked. For while we are still in this tent, we groan, being burdened—not that we would be unclothed, but that we would be further clothed, so that what is mortal may be swallowed up by life. (2 Corinthians 5:1–4)

Hope clothes our bodies. It covers the shame of sexual sin, self-harm, obesity. It covers the embarrassment of our physical symptoms of illness and clothes the side effects of medications that help us, albeit imperfectly. Our bodies are continuously impacted by disintegration and death, but because of Jesus, they are *more* greatly impacted by *Jesus'* death. When we hold His grace next to our brokenness, His grace is always bigger. Because of Jesus, our story isn't physical disintegration until death; instead, it is healing and life each day, even as we age and fight an onslaught of physical challenges in our brokenness. We are renewed day by day in Christ's hope. When we awake, we can acknowledge His care that brought us our breath for another day. When we are confused, we turn to Him and find insight and strength. Then one day, when we take our final breath, we will find ourselves free of brokenness, looking into His eyes, meeting Him face-to-face. We will find hope in eternity, bolder and brighter, but the same hope we found in Him each day before.

> For I know that my Redeemer lives,
>> and at the last He will stand upon the earth.
> And after my skin has been thus destroyed,
>> yet in my flesh I shall see God,
> whom I shall see for myself,
>> and my eyes shall behold, and not another.
> My heart faints within me! (Job 19:25–27)

EMOTION

emotion

1 a conscious or unconscious internal state related to processing our experiences and relationships through external and internal input

If I had to use one word to describe the concept of emotion, I would use *complex*. In this broken world, we do not usually experience emotions with precision; they're layered and vague, which can be confusing and even painful. They can feel out of our control. Emotions begin well below the surface of our consciousness, so that by the time I acknowledge that I'm feeling frustrated, I have probably been frustrated for ten minutes already and am well on my way to anger. It can be challenging to find language for the emotions we are feeling at any given time. Brokenness also complicates and distorts our ability to sense and name our emotions, limiting our awareness of the sensations that belong to the emotions inside of us. An emotion that was only hanging out, nagging us mildly, can suddenly overwhelm us, and we might not recognize other, underlying emotions. Our anger, our happiness, our contentment can be tinged with sadness, disappointment, or loneliness.

Our emotions are a full-body experience—not limited to our hearts or processes in our brains. We experience emotions heart, soul, mind, and strength. Our bodies bring in information through our sensory and other systems, which is one reason we often refer to emotions as feelings. Our brains process this information, usually outside of our recognition, connecting the new information to what our body already knows from previous experiences and memories. Our sensory systems and neural circuitry make more connections. Sometimes these neural pathways move information in such a way to create thoughts that make us aware of the process. The multifaceted concept of emotion refers to this entire experience.

This physical experience of how we process emotions is also affected by brokenness. Our minds will miss information and cues. We are limited in our perspective. Our amygdala and related systems sense relational or emotional danger or uncertainty and encourage us to self-protect rather than to connect.[2]

We also experience our emotions within relationship with others much of the time, and we struggle to know how to handle those emotional interchanges well. We don't always perceive or interpret another person's emotion accurately or at all! We miss their cues, both verbal and nonverbal. Our own experiences and beliefs about emotions heavily influence this elucidation and interpretation. For instance, while we rarely tell someone directly that their sadness is unacceptable, we offer very few places where it is emotionally and relationally safe to be sad. We try to fix and solve and escape these uncomfortable emotions at all costs. When we try to hold our emotions outside of our awareness, never considering or examining them, we can feel disconnected and isolated. And if we don't talk about emotions in our families or faith communities, then when we open our Bibles and find God's anger or sadness, we can be confused and scared to ask questions for fear of experiencing more disconnection, more brokenness.

On our journey toward emotional awareness, we must first wrestle with the concept of emotions themselves and where they come from. With that foundation in place, we can tackle our *experience* of those emotions. Take a minute to ask yourself: Where (or who) do emotions come from? Do they have a useful purpose? If so, what do we believe their purpose is?

As in all things, we turn to the Bible to find our foundation. First, Colossians 1:15–17 tells us God creates all things and all things were created for Him and through Him. That "all" includes abstract concepts such as our emotions. Because what God creates is good, we know emotions themselves are good gifts from God. Anything God creates for good, Satan will twist for evil. We sometimes see only the brokenness and evil within our emotions, but they were good and only good first, and they remain good, yet tainted by sin and brokenness.

Second, God Himself is an emotional being. Emotions are part of His image and His character. One benefit of emotions, and perhaps one of their greatest purposes, is that they connect humanity to God. This is made clear throughout the Bible.

- God is joyful. "The joy of the Lord" is our strength, according to Nehemiah 8:10. In John 15:11, Jesus remarks on sharing His joy with His followers.

- God also experiences anger and jealousy toward His people. This does not impact His holiness. In God's anger and jealousy, He is still righteous. We see examples of God's anger in Lamentations, Ezekiel, Isaiah, and

Jeremiah, particularly when God's people are unfaithful. We also see Jesus' human yet divine expression of anger in Mark 3:1–6.

- God expresses sadness over the sin and brokenness of this world. When humankind was at its worst, before the flood of Genesis, Scripture says "it grieved Him to His heart" (Genesis 6:6). Jesus famously wept at Lazarus's death, recorded in John 11:35.

These examples (and many others) show how God connects with His creation through emotions and models emotion for humans. In acknowledging both the joy of life and the sadness of brokenness, God gives us the freedom to acknowledge our own sadness in the broken things and experiences of this life. Yet it's important to note that God experiences emotions in perfection, fully integrated; we experience them in imperfection. In a fully integrated world, we would experience each emotion the way it was intended to be experienced. Instead, our experience of emotions in this life is very much imperfect.

You can likely list some emotions you'd rather be rid of. For many of us, sadness, fear, anger, hopelessness, and rage might top the list. But in brokenness, even these challenging emotions have a purpose. While we may not have been created *for* fear or sadness, I do believe we were created with the ability to experience fear and sadness. How else would we process loss in a broken world? How else would we be alerted to the dangers all around us? How else would we fight injustice? Fear, sadness, and anger all have their place in a broken world. Once sin and brokenness came in, we would need fear as an internal warning light. We would need anger for expressing our hurt. We would need tears to release the sadness within us.

But for now, we walk a broken journey with an unbreakable Savior.

We can turn toward God in every one of our emotions, rather than giving in to the temptation to turn away from God when we experience challenging emotions. God promises the restoration of all things when He comes back for us. There will be a time when anger is no more and tears are a thing of our past. But for now, we walk a broken journey with an unbreakable Savior. Jesus' presence in our lives brings hope for both today and tomorrow. When we look around and see hurt, evil, and injustice, God's perfect love has the power to transform. When we see hurt, evil, and injustice in our own hearts and lives, in Jesus, God brings healing to us. Through Jesus' sacrifice and kindness to us, and the Holy Spirit's continual presence, God is integrating and restoring us every day until Jesus comes again and makes everything new.

That process of daily integration—of God's healing with a side of life's heartbreak—feels messy though. We want perfection in everything *now*—including our emotions. When we are honest, we want the feel-good stuff without the uncomfortable stuff. We want continual goodness, happiness, joyfulness, contentment, and gratitude now. But God brought us here to this earth capable of feeling the uncomfortable emotions we'd rather throw away. He isn't intimidated by them. Turning toward God instead of away from God, especially in the uncomfortable emotions, brings hope into our discomfort. Uncomfortable emotions show us our need and the world's need for help, for forgiveness, and for God. As humans, we want to control our experience—in with the "good" emotions and out with the "bad" emotions. In our broken understanding, we settle for counterfeit clarity and half-truths. God instead gives fullness to our human experience.

Good and bad are overly simple categories for complex concepts. Good and bad are concrete, objective adjectives, which makes them especially difficult to apply to the very subjective experience of emotions. While sadness might *feel* bad, God does not call it bad in Scripture. It is an important distinction that emotions themselves are not sinful. In our brokenness, we can do sinful things *with* our emotions, like nursing frustration and disappointment to become bitterness or allowing happiness to be the god of our life, following it every which way it might lead. We can also allow emotions to feed sinful thoughts. When we let our emotions lead us, rather than inform us, we end up in a puddle of guilt, weighed down by our hurtful, aggressive, or selfish words and actions. It's important for our spiritual and emotional health to honestly confront these rather than turning them into blame or shame, both of which further point us inward, instead of pointing us to God.

With emotions as with all things, we let God do the work of telling us *who we are*. We are not how we feel, just as we are not what we do or what we think. We are God's children, loved, forgivable, capable of much good and much hurt. Our emotions make terrible foundations for our day. When we judge our life and ourselves by them, our identity will feel like a roller coaster. You are not your sadness. You are not your happiness. You are more than your momentary emotions. You are a much-loved child of God. Jesus Christ died so that your identity is also redeemed, rescued, and set free. We can acknowledge the brokenness of the world and within ourselves without making "broken" our entire identity. Take heart; your identity is secure in the Creator who made you and the Savior who died for you. There is no brokenness God cannot repair—this is a foundation of hope.

We also begin to build our emotional awareness. We recognize our emotions as God-given gifts and pay attention to them, as we would any gift from God. Because we have so many emotions that seem to pop up unbidden on a daily basis, most of us handle them by wrangling them like cattle or sheep. In our attempts to control our emotions, we usually default to one of three things: stuffing them down, shoving them out onto others, or ignoring them completely.

We stuff down our emotions when we feel the first niggling sensation of an emotion and respond by acknowledging it but pretending it isn't true or has no impact on our thoughts, bodies, or behaviors. Many of us become pretty adept at this. When we see an emotion, we wrangle it and stuff it way down deep inside ourselves, hiding it from those who love us and even from our own brain. When we refuse to give our emotions any space for observation or any voice for information, our bodies take the brunt of them, holding stress, tension, and inflammation. Research shows that our immune system is affected by our emotions in many ways, and vice versa.[3] As more research comes out on emotions and immunology, we see more clearly how God knit together our internal systems. Giving ourselves space to acknowledge and express emotions, without letting them dictate our decisions, can be powerful for our health. The physical and mental burden of emotions is overwhelming at times, but because Christ made a way for our salvation, the Holy Spirit inhabits this body too.

Letting our emotions have room doesn't mean the Holy Spirit has left or will leave us. We call on that same Spirit as we reveal our emotions to ourselves, to God, and to one another.

Shoving our emotions onto others happens when we feel the discomfort of an emotion (or several emotions at one time) but don't deal with it personally, and it ends up boiling over into our relationships. Emotions left undealt with over time often end up taking the form of blame, shame, judgment, or cynicism. Emotions are not leaders. We get into trouble when we allow them to be our guides for how we interact with others. We all need help sorting out ourselves and sorting out our lives, including our emotions. The Holy Spirit is our Counselor; God's Word is our guide. They speak truth, love, and hope into us and our relationships when our emotions speak all sorts of other things.

We also get into trouble when we ignore our emotions completely. This is different than stuffing them down, because we never felt them in the first place. The problem is that we have to numb ourselves in order to ignore our emotions. We can't numb only the emotions we like or don't like. Our brains and bodies don't work that way. So we have to numb everything. We sort of shut down. We end up cut off from ourselves and one another, even from God. Numb is no way to live. And unfortunately, emotions that go unrecognized and unnoticed will make themselves known in one way or another, and that often results in dangerous or sinful words and actions.

Another reason we call emotions "feelings" is because we can "feel" them moving around inside our bodies and our inward being—our hearts, our souls, our perceptions. Research shows the higher the *granularity* and *differentiation* we have for our emotions, the more likely we are to be able to experience those emotions in health.[4] Granularity is our ability to give words to our emotions, the process of bringing them to light. Giving our emotions names and a voice helps us connect heart to mind and ignite our will, given to us by God, to regulate our emotions. The closer we can get to naming and describing an emotion in detail, the more likely we are to regulate it in line with our values and beliefs. Differentiation, on the other hand, is the process of recognizing and distinguishing our own emotions from someone else's. Because relationships are important, even vital, this can be difficult work. We can mistake loving someone with holding their emotions for them. We pick up the anxiety someone is expressing or not expressing in a conversation. We feed off the joy they are experiencing or the discontent they are wrestling with. Some of this contagion sounds just lovely, but it's better for our emotional and spiritual health to be honest and authentic, sharing our emotions with one another in the open, rather than misunderstanding mine for yours and yours for mine.

God did design emotions to connect us to other human beings. Feeling someone else's emotions, while distinguishing them from our own experience, is what we call empathy. Empathy is an awesome and healthy form of emotional sharing. Scripture reminds us to suffer and rejoice together (1 Corinthians 12:26). This healthy sharing in the form of empathy binds, knits, and heals broken hearts and broken lives by the power of the Holy Spirit. When I returned to therapy this year with only a sense of sadness, a fair amount of anger, and a knotted ball of unanswered questions and unstated struggle in my stomach, my therapist helped me unravel the ball by giving me a safe place to say my fears out loud and assisted me in naming my overflowing emotions. She helped me define and name the emotions within my experience. She provided the warmth of empathy to do this work. In this work, I could more clearly see the stability of Jesus in the instability of my emotions. That stability translated to my heart and mind as hope.

We are always invited to lay before Christ the chaos inside of us and all around us. Brokenness may press in, but God remains closer within us. In Christ, we never have to reflect on our joy or our heartbreak alone. Naming an emotion brings light to subjects that can feel confusing, dark, or overwhelming. The light of Christ will always bring hope into brokenness. Psalm 139:1–3 assures us:

> O LORD, You have searched me and known me!
> You know when I sit down and when I rise up;
>   You discern my thoughts from afar.
> You search out my path and my lying down
>   and are acquainted with all my ways.

He knows all of us, including our emotions, and still wants to know us more. He is with us as we discern all the messy processes inside of us. Psalm 139 concludes by acknowledging the uncomfortable emotions we experience because we see brokenness in us and around us:

> Search me, God, and know my heart;
>   test me and know my anxious thoughts.
> See if there is any offensive way in me,
>   and lead me in the way everlasting. (vv. 23–24, NIV)

This is hope: God offers redemption to our whole selves in Jesus Christ. Jesus brings us salvation but also transforms the shape of everything in our lives—our emotions included. God sees every shout of excitement and every moment of brooding, every peal of laughter and every valley of broken hopelessness. Our gentle Savior is with us no matter what we feel. When we confess God's promises alongside our broken reality, He brings light to every subject. Our emotions are touched by brokenness, but they are transformed by Hope.

RESILIENCE

resilience

1 the capability to come back from a struggle with renewed hope, life, and a greater ability to respond to future stressors

2 the internal capacity of people to recover, gaining new insights, strengths, and capabilities we did not have before a struggle

Resilience is a hot commodity in our modern world. Even when we don't have language for brokenness, people can see the mess of this life around them. In the United States, we love victory. When we live in a culture that loves victory, we naturally look for ways to conquer or overcome the mess. For the most part, humanity jointly recognizes that the mess doesn't seem to be going anywhere anytime soon. But we do want answers and solutions to the mess. Insert resilience.

Resilience is often defined as bouncing or springing back when battered by suffering or hardship—emphasizing the ability of a person or thing to "get back to normal" or return to a former shape. This definition is good for memory foam pillows and stress balls. When I squish a stress ball, it regains its size and shape pretty quickly. But when we apply this definition to people, we relate resilience not to their growth but to their ability to respond to stresses that require adjustment. I take issue with definitions that make resilience sound so *easy*. Because we are complex and whole people—body, mind, and spirit—our resilience is more complex than that of a stress ball.

Resilience comes only in struggle's wake.

Resilience comes only in struggle's wake. Anyone displaying attributes of resilience has fought for that resilience, often through struggle, suffering, or trauma. When we miss this fighting component of resilience, we also miss God entering into the hard places of our lives and working in them. Resilience, when applied to people and not foam, requires a definition that acknowledges the challenges brokenness brings into our lives and honors the efforts of walking through those struggles. For Christians, resilience also means relying on the gift of God's grace as the agent of transformation in life.

God did create human creatures with an ability to recover from hard things. And yet we also develop this ability to recover throughout our lives. For example, parents build resilience into their children by giving them independence to walk through their own struggles while also offering support and love. Resilience is a gift of God's Spirit working in us, but that work of God's grace often looks like a gritty battle, with nights of questions and wrestling, building a stick-to-itiveness over time. How do we get to more of the hope resilience brings into our lives? There is no step-by-step plan for resilience, but we start by recognizing God's faithfulness not only in the good things of life but also in the valleys and deserts. Then, we can identify the skills that build resilience, such as naming our emotions, being aware of our problems, discerning which steps to take to overcome those problems, and asking for help.

The apostle Paul, writer of many of the New Testament letters, was no stranger to resilience or trauma. He dealt over and over again with other people's sin heaped on him. He was thrown into prison by leaders who didn't want to acknowledge their own need. He was excluded and slandered by individuals and whole communities. He was beaten for sharing hope with those desperately in need of it. Yet he expresses strength and heartbreak in the same breath in each of his letters. He was resilient in acknowledging his own sin—identifying himself as chief of sinners (1 Timothy 1:15)—and encouraging those he mentored and led to recognize their need for Christ and forgiveness.

Brokenness was a heavy reality for Paul, and it's a heavy reality for us too. The world is disintegrating, groaning for God to come and restore it. The challenges of life quite literally break the world apart. In our state of brokenness, we are pushed and pulled to our limits. The brokenness inside of us and in our families eats away at our sense of worth and our ability to believe we are lovable or that forgiveness is possible. Sometimes we don't feel or see resilience in our lives. And unfortunately, some lives seem to get a double portion of the trauma that comes with brokenness. How do people keep going when they've been abused? How do we battle against the nightmares of our past or help someone battle their personal nightmares without buckling under the weight of brokenness? How does someone trust again after being betrayed? How do we recover from the heartache when our relationships are destroyed, sometimes by our own hand?

We start by calling brokenness by name and recognizing that resilience is really brokenness but with hope attached.

The New Testament uses the language of an athletic race to help us see both the place of resilience in our lives and God's work *building* resilience in us.

The New Testament uses the language of an athletic race to help us see both the place of resilience in our lives and God's work *building* resilience in us. Psychological research reveals what the Bible started teaching long ago—that hope and resilience are intimately connected.[5] The Bible's version of hope, however, is a more resilient form of resilience! Our resilience in Christ is based on an unchanging God, rather than on our ever-changing human vantage point of this world. But until we see Christ face-to-face, He uses other faces to speak His hope over us: we are not alone in this race. Brokenness often clouds our hope, but when we gather around God's Word, reminding one another of the Hope inside of us, we build resilience together. Other people, their support, God's affection, God's presence in His Word and by His Spirit— these all help us learn resilience as we walk through struggles in hope. Hebrews 12:1–2 reminds us that no matter what our race looks like, every one of us has the God of the universe plotting the course, as well as fellow runners and a cheering section:

> Therefore, since we are surrounded by so great a cloud
> of witnesses, let us also lay aside every weight, and sin
> which clings so closely, and let us run with endurance
> the race that is set before us, looking to Jesus, the
> founder and perfecter of our faith, who for the joy that
> was set before him endured the cross, despising the

shame, and is seated at the right hand of the throne of
God.

The Book of Romans shows the connection between resilience and throwing off the ankle weights of sin and shame in this
race:

> We rejoice in hope of the glory of God. Not only that,
> but we rejoice in our sufferings, knowing that suffering
> produces endurance, and endurance produces charac-
> ter, and character produces hope, and hope does not
> put us to shame, because God's love has been poured
> into our hearts through the Holy Spirit who has been
> given to us. For while we were still weak, at the right
> time Christ died for the ungodly. (5:2–6)

Throwing off shame is important to the concept of resilience.
We fix our eyes on Jesus not only when we are tempted by sin but
also when shame threatens to trip us up. Shame says, "You can't
do it. You will never make it. There's no one cheering for you.
God went home a long time ago." Romans speaks truth when the
voices of shame grow loud. Look ahead to the finish line. Jesus
stands there, present, not far off or disinterested. We look into
His eyes and see hope blazing brightly. We look all around us and
see the faces of His people, who are also throwing off their ankle
weights of sin and shame. Those same people are also the crowd,
handing us those tiny cups of water to keep us going. They hold
signs decorated with streamers that say, "Keep at it, dear one!"
and "Child of God, that is who you are!" These things bring the
bounce and the spring into our lives. The louder our people cheer
for us and invest in us, the easier it is to block out the voices that

tear us down, and the harder it is to ignore the voices of hope and resilience. Resilience is infinitely harder without the Savior and without the crowd.

Hopelessness weighs down. But hope builds up. How can we share hope?

Resilience is not about finding easy answers for overcoming. Brokenness can feel like a hike through the densest jungle without a machete, even in faith. Yet faith in Jesus does give us feet that can move forward. As we do so, it's important to have compassion on other Christians, but also and especially on those who don't know Jesus in this broken world. Can you imagine how hard it must be to move forward in resilience without the hope of restoration? Even in Christ, we are prone to cover up our pain. We try to numb the hurts of this life with addictions or the pleasures of the moment. We turn inward. We isolate and push against meaningful relationships that might help us. In a life without the hope of faith, the battle is tenfold. Hopelessness weighs down. But hope builds up. How can we share hope? How can we bring compassion for ourselves and for others because of God's compassion for us? Be assured, God is continually working integration into us, which helps us to adapt in our circumstances and see options for our future—that is, to be resilient.

My redemption is never dependent on my resilience. I am saved by Christ alone. Resilience is the good fight through the brokenness of life. Resilience is getting up in the morning, sometimes only by the grace of God, grabbing His hand, and believing that Jesus and I can do this new day together. In resilience, I can stand in brokenness and still see hope, even when it feels far away. Some days, I might need your help so I can see hope, but I know it's always there. This is hope: There will be days of doubt and days of trust, and most days will include both. We will have questions, and God will hear them because Christ opened that door for us long ago when He came into this world to save us. The Father, the Son, and the Spirit can handle our traumas. Our God can handle our questions.

Hope echoes within us the words of Paul in 2 Timothy 4:7: "I have fought the good fight, I have finished the race, I have kept the faith." And then we say it again the next morning and the next. We say it to the believers around us and remind them that we are their cheering section. We raise a banner of hope in Christ for the world all around us. We raise it over the darkness and the brokenness we see everywhere. The hope of Christ fills our hearts, our minds, our lungs, and our muscles to run through the brokenness toward restoration. His promises are our strength.

VULNERABILITY

vulnerability

1 an uncomfortable emotion experienced within relationship because of our internal sensation of exposure and our own uncertainty of others' responses

2 the natural state of existing in need of God and desiring relationship with Him

When I was a little girl, I was very aware of my smallness. I wore child's size six dresses and pants until I was ten years old. When I held my dad's hand as we crossed a parking lot, I remember noticing his calloused work hands and how infinitely big they felt in comparison to my own. As a member of what we might call the "Stranger Danger" generation, I was constantly reminded that I was vulnerable, that life in this big world came with risk.

My family also showed me that there is lots of adventure to be had in this life. We went to museums and neighbors' homes and explored the woods behind our house. My parents acknowledged the dangers of life but at the same time allowed for the risks that come with any adventure and any relationship. They taught the juxtaposition of risk and caution in words and actions, which left me with a sense of comfort in my vulnerability. As a trauma therapist, I am aware that this is a luxury not all children get to enjoy. On top of that, my parents have always been appropriately honest about their own brokenness and the brokenness they have encountered in their lives. For this, I am forever grateful.

Search the internet for the word *vulnerability*, and you will get a million terrible definitions. These definitions often imply that vulnerability is a state we choose to place ourselves in—vulnerable or not vulnerable. Other definitions equate vulnerability with the likelihood of someone being wounded, attacked, or harmed—which positions us to view vulnerability through a negative lens. I think these definitions come from a place of hurt and brokenness. Without the safety of God's arms to catch us, being vulnerable sounds awful. While we certainly can choose whether to lean into vulnerability, these definitions overemphasize controlling it. We want vulnerability to be a choice, something we can engage in or disengage from. This allows us to feel like we can protect ourselves from vulnerability as we would protect ourselves from snakes, hurricanes, or robbers. We believe we can lock the doors of our psyches, our hearts, and our lives to keep trouble at bay. But brokenness will always find its way in, like dust and pollen find their way into houses locked up tight.

We have always been and will always be vulnerable, because we are human.

We have always been and will always be vulnerable, because we are human.

The best definition I have found for vulnerability comes from the research of Brené Brown, who offers a clear and simple definition in her book *Daring Greatly*. She acknowledges that vulnerability is complex but limits the definition to these essential elements, which emerged over her years of research: "uncertainty, risk, and emotional exposure."[6]

Let me clarify that people experience all kinds of vulnerability—physical, intellectual, relational, financial, and more. However, all of these experiences of vulnerability funnel to the *emotional experience* of it, which feels to our body, mind, and spirit like exposure. But beyond an emotional experience, perhaps at its core vulnerability is a spiritual experience.

Unwrap vulnerability with me by going back to the very beginning. In Genesis 1, God creates the whole universe, and then in Genesis 2, God creates man and woman and calls them "very good." It's quite clear that there was a time when Adam and Eve walked around with God, talked with God, and interacted in harmony with the natural world around them every day without any of the brokenness we experience. Just before the fall into sin comes the last verse of Genesis 2. Genesis 2:25 is short and easily skipped over: "And the man and his wife were both naked and were not ashamed."

Adam and Eve were naked. They weren't only naked because they were marriage partners (although that's a great takeaway about vulnerability and marriage that we'll dive into in the section on brokenness in families). Adam was also naked with God before Eve ever entered the picture. Eve was naked with God outside of Adam's presence. We all exist naked before God in every way—spiritually, emotionally, physically. Job 1:21 states, "Naked I came from my mother's womb, and naked shall I return." We, as humans, were all created *vulnerable* before God in this sense. The difference between Adam and Eve's Genesis 2 experience of nakedness and our own today? Shame. Without the possibility of shame, vulnerability has no risk and no uncertainty.

That leads us to this distinction: vulnerability exists without our perception of it. Vulnerability is not the result of sin. Because God is God—great, mighty, awesome, the Creator of everything, including us—we as humanity exist vulnerable as not-God. We are smaller, different from God, under God's authority. Because He is God and we are not, we have existed in vulnerability since the beginning, and we will be vulnerable to God in eternity. We were created to be naked and exposed but without shame. Can you imagine our experiences without the uncertainty we feel because of the brokenness of this world? Living without that uncertainty will be one of the great glories of our relationship with God when He restores all things.

The *risk* of vulnerability comes with the entrance of shame into this world. After Genesis 2:25 comes Genesis 3. The very first verse introduces us to the serpent and all his craftiness. When sin crashes into the world, we become suddenly aware of our vulnerability. In Genesis 3:7, one of the consequences of sin is shame, which changes our experience of vulnerability. The consequence of brokenness is a shame-filled awareness of our vulnerability. Without Christ lifting our shame, healing our shame, we see only our nakedness, and we are displeased. We look around and see that life with one another and our relationship with God are shattered at our feet.

Shame is now the common experience of humanity, handed down generation after generation since Genesis 3. Our new broken senses perceive only the lack, the weakness, the reality of our imperfection before a perfect God. The goodness of vulnerability can be hard for us to believe because we've only experienced it in brokenness. We wonder what would happen if God and those we love truly saw us. We live in the uncertainty of vulnerability, the weight of vulnerability, rather than its freedom. Shame is now the common experience of humanity, handed down generation after generation since Genesis 3. And then there's the devil and his schemes. In brokenness and outside of Christ, we are unprotected. Where do we turn? Where do we go to be safe? We bear this consequence of brokenness, all of us, ever since that day in Genesis 3. We turn away from relationships toward isolation because we are afraid of what someone will see in us. We get cozy in what is familiar and push against reasonable risk because failure breathes down our neck. We hide from God, pretending we don't need Him, He doesn't see us, or He doesn't exist.

God responds to the mess that lies broken at our feet and to the sadness that seeps in when we look at the shattered pieces we have no idea how to repair.

God steps in.

God is not vulnerable because He is God. There is no uncertainty or risk for Him. It's worth noting that He does experience hurt and sadness, yet steps in anyway. Scripture tells us of God's heartbreak over humanity's various rejections of Him, but He steps in. When we are the ones to reject Him, when we go against Him, when we hurt Him, God steps in. In His perfection, God is not guided by His sadness or anger. He is guided by Himself, which is both love and justice, fitting together in completeness.

This is hope: God steps in. For Adam and Eve then and for us now. God steps into our mess and calls us out of hiding.

Christ came so that our relationship with God could be reconciled by His cross. Yes, we're vulnerable and aware of that vulnerability in a new way in our brokenness. But if the God of the universe can call me out of hiding through His love and sacrifice, how can I not live outside of hiding? Vulnerability is not a dirty word, because it is God's word and it is good. Brokenness brings uncertainty. Every day we live trying to hide from our mistakes. Every day we live trying to hide from ourselves and God—tucking away the things we don't want to think about and revealing only what feels safe, even to ourselves. But God steps in. God sent Jesus as the substitute payment to fix the world that humanity shattered. God heard our sadness and our shame and sent Jesus. Jesus stepped in further, becoming man, taking on our clothes of vulnerability and wearing them around for thirty-three years. Jesus died on the cross to carry all shame so we never have to bear it again. He offered Himself as a vulnerable sacrifice so we could be covered and step into relationship with God once again.

God is more involved in our lives than we can imagine. With Christ as our Brother and Intercessor, God asks us questions and delves deeper into our lives. God in His mercy invites us to step into conversation with Him. He challenges us to consider the state of our sin, our disintegration, our brokenness. Jesus' death and resurrection provide a way to walk through the mess and brokenness, not around it. I can be vulnerable with myself and with other people in this life because I have a God who covers my uncertainty. Confession is a place to share not only our brokenness but the basic vulnerability of our existence too: "God, I need You. Jesus, I don't want to live without You. Spirit, make Your home here, so my awareness of You is bigger than my awareness of brokenness." People who do not know Jesus will have an even harder time stepping into this vulnerability. Without knowing the covering that's available to them, it will naturally be harder to step in, to invest, to look uncertainty and risk in the eye. I don't believe it's impossible, but it will be much, much harder. This should give us a level of compassion and gentleness in our relationships with those who do not know Him or His covering.

Once again, there are no easy answers in a broken world. Hope helps us see farther, to what is not immediately in front of us, so that we can find more hope in the midst of what is immediately in front of us. Jesus will completely renew us and all creation when He comes back to finish God's restoration plan, but until then, we still live in this broken world. Vulnerability will often continue to feel like exposure and uncertainty. But the hope of Jesus does change our understanding and experience of vulnerability. In Jesus, we have our foundation; there is no risk or uncertainty in our relationship with God, even in our nakedness. Jesus takes our hand so we can be vulnerable in this life. We can lean into vulnerability now, not because we experience it in perfection, but because relationships are worth the risk. We can be honest about ourselves, our complexities, and our struggles.

In Christ, we can walk together in hope.

MESSES IN FAMILY: BROKEN INTIMACY

intimacy

1 a depth of relationship, often reflected interpersonally as a sense of well-being and safety

2 a relational state that includes a sense of being deeply known—of someone knowing us inside and out, the strengths and the flaws, and offering us unconditional love with intentional accountability

God's Word is designed for us to clearly see Christ first in every verse, on every page, every time. Because Christ is both our redemption and our restoration, Scripture is also concerned with our relationships and our experiences of relationship in this life. God created intimacy for our health, to take our relationships beyond shallow connection. But because brokenness touches everything, it will touch all our places of relationship and intimacy too.

Our families are impacted by brokenness just as our individual bodies, minds, and souls are. We will experience brokenness as individuals, but also as family units. Still, God cares for families, just as He cares for individuals. He does not leave or forsake your family (Deuteronomy 31:6; Hebrews 13:5–6).

Because we stand with one foot in this broken world and one foot in the promise of God's restoration, we wrestle with the way brokenness and restoration interact in every sphere of our lives. Jesus is our individual foundation, but we also want to understand what it means for Him to be the foundation of our families. We start by asking foundational questions of God: What is family? What is its purpose? Where is God's hope, healing, and restoration for our most intimate relationships?

Jesus is our individual foundation, but we also want to understand what it means for Him to be the foundation of our families.

Part of the impact of brokenness is that some mysteries of God will remain until He comes again. While all we need to know has been revealed in Christ Jesus, 1 Corinthians also reminds us that the Spirit is forever digging with us to understand more (1 Corinthians 2:1–10; see also Colossians 1:24–26). Concepts such as intimacy and relationship are in that "more" category. We need insight from God on these things, and He gives it, but in doses, in stops and starts, in mercy and in growth. It is easy to forget the foundation of family and relationships when we are in the middle of all the work of family and relationships. It's hard for me to actively concern myself with the concepts of intimacy and safety when there are so many dirty water glasses and so much old homework to pick up. It's even harder for us to care about these abstract things when we're hurting from the sting of an argument or when estrangement, adultery, divorce, or abuse are part of our experience and lens for family life.

God created people and families all on the sixth day of creation. God the Father created humans with His own hands, and then He presented Eve to Adam to create the first family. The name *Eve* means "mother of all the living," and so through this first family, generation after generation of families would come (Genesis 2:4). Genesis 2:25 applies to God's desires for our sense of identity in Christ, naked and without shame, and also to our sense of identity as a family that God has knit together.

Families were and are intended to be the relational places in our lives where we could be most intimate and known. Then, brokenness came in and shattered things, including relationships and intimacy. With brokenness, we also need a place in our lives where we can have a greater sense of safety, because the world is no longer the safe place we had in the Garden of Eden. Christ is our truest safe place. He knows us and loves us most intimately. But God gives more grace, and that grace includes other intimate relationships.

God continues to create intimacy by creating marriage and by introducing family as fruitful. Marriage is part of intimacy, but it isn't all there is of intimacy. Children are part of intimacy, but they aren't all there is to intimacy either. We'll get to the other places of intimacy God creates for us—friendship, the Body of Christ, and more—in the next section. But first, let's stay with the concept of family intimacy and explore more of Genesis 2 and 3 together. What does intimacy look like after brokenness entered in Genesis 3? How can we identify the brokenness and chaos of our own family while holding tightly to hope and grace?

SAFETY AND KNOWING

safety

1 a perceived sense of protection

2 an emotionally significant sense of protection or covering in our life that comes from having relationships that include both unconditional love and accountability

knowing

1 a state of deep intimacy, including a sense of awareness that one is seen as a whole person

2 a relational state in which all parts of one's character—experiences, thoughts, feelings, and behaviors—are perceived as a whole

We all come from families and continue to be touched by family life throughout our lives. Families come in all shapes and sizes, with all kinds of support and also all kinds of brokenness. What kind of brokenness can you identify in your own experience of living within a family? I have noticed that sometimes the chaos of brokenness looks kind of average. Each family deals daily with household-chore arguments and run-of-the-mill who did what, where, and when, and who failed to show up and do x, y, and z. But sometimes brokenness in families isn't so average; it can also be shocking or traumatic. No matter how it barges in, brokenness means that relationships will always be work, especially our most intimate ones.

Brokenness means that relationships will always be work, especially our most intimate ones.

Two concepts show up consistently when studying relational intimacy in the Bible: safety and knowing. Genesis 3:16–19 helps us to understand the work and struggle of creating safety and knowing in our relationships in this broken world. The sweat and toil of work was part of the curse of humankind when brokenness entered into the world. In the intimacy of family life, we take on that sweat and toil together in close quarters, where the stakes seem highest because the people matter to us most. In Genesis 3:16–19, we are also given the curse of pain in childbearing and the tension of our competing desires for someone to care for us and to be in control ourselves. We feel the weight and pressure of brokenness in our family life. There is pain in parenting beyond labor. Families struggle to understand who should lead and make decisions in any given situation. We want to understand our roles in family life, just as we want to understand our purpose in this world in general. God restores our families and integrates our relationships with one another in Christ Jesus, but that sense of disintegration from brokenness and its curse will also still be there. God's creation of relationship and families is beautiful and full of joy, but that doesn't make it less hard.

There was a time when the whole world was safe, before brokenness. Then, in sin, Adam and Eve were cast out of complete safety—both the physical place of safety where they resided, the Garden of Eden, and their relational safety with God. We live in this brokenness to this day. Our families are like islands in the giant ocean of life and its vastness. It is a biblical and scientific reality that we cannot expect true intimacy and safety among all 7.5 billion people of this world. We cannot know and be known deeply by 7.5 billion people. God gave us families. Families are where the heavy lifting of growing and developing happens; we return to those relationships again and again as they point us to Jesus, reminding us that we belong and have a place in this gigantic broken universe.

The term *knowing* is used in Scripture to describe having knowledge, as in information or understanding, but also having a depth of intimacy in relationship. The Old Testament describes sexual intimacy using this term. We see the impact of brokenness and heartbreak most clearly and boldly when we mess with God's plans for sexual intimacy, partly because that special type of intimacy overflows into intimacy of all kinds. Sex is a good gift, but many of us are familiar with the rending of hearts and lives that comes with our own sexual sin. Far too many of us are also familiar with the trauma of sexual sin placed on us by someone else in rape or sexual abuse.[7] Shards of broken intimacy are all around us—human trafficking, sexualized television programs geared toward children (or anyone), the suggestion that abortion has no cost, no grief, no heartache. The weight of brokenness and shame is particularly heavy in this area. When we talk about sexual sin with a tone of compassion, I think we can be heard more clearly. We accurately call brokenness by name when we recognize the deep impact sexual sin has on humanity as a whole, stealthily moving from generation to generation.

But terms for *know* or *knowing* in Scripture are not limited to intellectual or sexual contexts. The Hebrew root word is used particularly in contexts of revealing something.[8] Intimacy—truly knowing and being known—is both revealing oneself and allowing someone else to reveal themselves. Intimacy is being seen by someone without chameleon masks or pretenses. God knows us and sees us thoroughly. Brokenness ruptured the intimacy we have with God as humans. The results are devastating. God wants to repair. God wants to reintegrate. God wants to heal. Even though brokenness is in every fiber of our being and every attempt we make at relationship, we are given the gift of knowing God through Jesus Christ. In Jesus, God also created a way for us to experience His heart of intimacy in relationship with one another.

Families may not be glamorous, and they may even be a big old mess in many ways. But brokenness didn't change the purpose of families—just the way we get there. Families are intended to be places where we can be known in intimacy, where we can grow with God and one another. Because brokenness is our reality, we also need safety, especially in intimate relationships. God gives us Christ as the person with whom we can be completely safe—emotionally, relationally. Have you noticed one-way intimacy never works out for long? This is true in both our relationship with Christ and our relationship in our families and beyond. Our relationship of knowing with Christ is reciprocal. He shows us Himself in His Word and offers Himself to be known uniquely in the Lord's Supper. Reciprocal intimacy isn't necessary for God to give us, but it is His desire for us because He is the Creator of intimacy. In our intimacy with Christ, we can walk into truly reciprocal intimacy with one another, and that starts in families.

As long as we exist in a broken world, brokenness will reside in families. Our families are imperfect. Some of our families are incredibly, horribly, devastatingly, destructively imperfect. Most of us will encounter a deeper sense of brokenness, a need to name the brokenness, within our families because of the deeper intimacy also found in families. This is hope in our most intimate relationships: In the imperfection of brokenness, it's obvious we need grace. Forgiveness builds a unique sense of safety and knowing into our relationships. At its core, family is a place of relationship where we can glimpse God's unconditional love in a very conditionally minded world.

CHILDHOOD

childhood

1 a time of rapid development and growth during which an individual experiences a unique formation into what various cultures and societies understand to be adulthood

2 the period of time when a young person is under the care of other individuals

We were all children once. We all have a backstory and a childhood. And we all grew up in what we call a family of origin—often referred to by its acronym, FOO, in therapy documents. I do especially like this acronym because saying "FOO" aloud brings some lightheartedness to a topic that often feels pretty heavy.

How do you feel about your FOO? I have learned that there is a universal truth we are all reticent to admit: some things about our family of origin will be good, and other things will be not so good. Some things will even be very good, and to varying degrees, many of us will also experience awful things in our family of origin. Jesus helps us to know our identity apart from our experiences. We have belonging in this life because we belong to God, our Father. When our families have not been places of safety, or when we experience moments of wrecked intimacy, we are still loved and treasured by God, whether child or adult. There is nothing that can separate us from His love. Knowing our identity *and* our belonging is firmly grounded in Him, we can begin to take an honest look at our family of origin.

God is the founder of all families and the Father of all families. Our earthly fathers and mothers will be imperfect, sometimes shockingly so. When we talk about the complications of childhood, we need to know that God not only placed us in our families but that He also knew brokenness would impact every family, so He sent Christ Jesus for them too. Listen to Ephesians 3:14–19 on families and Jesus:

> For this reason I bow my knees before the Father, from whom every family in heaven and on earth is named, that according to the riches of His glory He may grant you to be strengthened with power through His Spirit in your inner being, so that Christ may dwell in your hearts through faith—that you, being rooted and grounded in love, may have strength to comprehend with all the saints what is the breadth and length and height and depth, and to know the love of Christ that surpasses knowledge, that you may be filled with all the fullness of God.

Families being named by God means He crafted each one of them into being. I am a Goehmann because God fit those pieces of my life together for me to carry that name. I am also a Weirich and a Kerkman because God fit other complicated bits of my broken life together and redeemed them in Christ. God knew we would be messy when He created the world. He knows we will be messy, and He still creates each of us and each of our families. He knows His grace can cover our brokenness and the places of our life where brokenness leans in nice and close.

God is sad when we hurt. Few things cause people as much hurt as the junky stuff they experienced as a child or continue to experience in their families today. Christ is the substitute who paid the price for all the brokenness we encounter, including the complex layers of brokenness in families. His death on the cross pays for our sin and also for the sins of our caregivers. That is a fact, whether all parties involved recognize it or not. Every sin and shame life could lob at us was nailed to the cross with Jesus. We confess the parts of brokenness that are our own sin, and Jesus heals those wounds. We also confess the parts of brokenness that are not our sins, and Jesus heals those wounds as well. Christ's healing for us does not depend on whether others see their part in the brokenness.

There are no "good childhoods" and "bad childhoods." There are only broken childhoods, touched by Hope or untouched by Hope. Calling our experiences of brokenness in our childhood by name doesn't negate the good parts of our childhood. A meal is more complete with both brussels sprouts and birthday cake. Christ loves families and sees them with mercy, in the same way He sees us as individuals through the lens of His mercy. He walks with us to help us see with eyes of love, without minimizing or hiding the brokenness of our experiences.

In the Old Testament, we find a heavy emphasis on family lineage in order to point to the long-awaited arrival of Jesus. I love that God includes details about these FOOs of Jesus and His grandparents and great-grandparents and so on. Even in the lineage of Jesus, we get a good look at family dynamics gone awry in brokenness: Abraham tried to pass his wife, Sarah, off as his sister to save his own shirt (twice!); Isaac and Rebekah played favorites; and Ruth encountered incredible loss, poverty, and disappointment in her life.

Jesus' family line is just as messy and chaotic as yours, I promise, but He remains the perfect Savior of the world. We want God to clean up our family messes of brokenness. Yet God didn't feel the need to clean up for Jesus. Families are made uniquely. They each have their own unique set of problems. Both in the Bible and in our world today, there are families who yell. There is jealousy. There is heartache and leaving. There is hugging and kissing. There is care and concern, as well as injustice. There is a lot of cooking and feeding. There are families who are ripped apart and families who are blended and pieced back together. Families have been wonderful and complicated since the beginning of time.

Childhood can hold some very deep wounds—traumas that impact us for a lifetime, even if others don't notice or if we ourselves don't recognize them. Those traumas are likely to occur within the context of family. The more intimate a relationship is, the more painful and influential it can be.

When we are young, we rely on the adults whom God has entrusted with our care. Psychologists refer to the miraculous neurological and relational work of these early relationships as attachment. The attachments formed when we are young lay the groundwork for the attachments we experience in relationships as we grow. The strength and consistency of our early attachments also develop our capacity for growth in other areas of our lives—our understanding of vulnerability, resilience, and intimacy. Healthy attachments are formed when infants and children get their needs met on a regular basis and learn that someone responds when they cry and ask for help, and when children are allowed to grow and gain independence as they get older and still find a place to land when they fall. Attachments can also bring healing. Later attachments in our lives can repair challenging attachments we might have had when we were young.

There is a spiritual foundation to attachment that often goes undernoticed in research. According to Psalm 139, God knit our bodies, minds, and spirits together in the womb. Miraculously, He also begins knitting our relationships and our senses of identity and belonging in that same womb and then throughout our lives.[9] When our caregivers respond to our needs, we learn in a mysterious way that God responds to our needs as well. When our caregivers treat us in ways that mirror the way God values us, a foundation is laid for an internal belief system that says we are worthy of love and honor, not because of how we perform, what we look like, or our family name, but because we are made lovingly by God.

Like all aspects of relationship, attachment isn't simple. There is a misconception that moms and dads have babies and then fall instantly in love with them. This puts a peculiar pressure on parents when brokenness leans in, when love takes work, and when they experience the exhaustion of new parenting or teen parenting. The safety of attachment between loved ones happens both naturally but also with effort. None of our early relationships will be perfect. Many attachments are interrupted by forces outside of our control—adoption, health complications during gestation or birth, early loss or trauma, and a parent's difficult experiences with attachment from their own childhood.

We rely on God to work attachment as He knits together our relationships, but we also put forth effort in attachment by being responsive in our relationships. This responsiveness is called attunement. There are likely areas of our relationships where our caregivers and loved ones have been very attuned and areas where they haven't. Brokenness impacts attachment, like it impacts everything else. But brokenness never gets the last word. Christ does.

Brokenness impacts attachment, like it impacts everything else. But brokenness never gets the last word. Christ does.

God gives us the ability to love, and it shows up in wild and wonderful ways, sometimes seemingly out of the blue. Yet secure attachment is that love supported by caregivers putting effort into understanding their child and getting to *know* their child, tuning in to them. Practicing attunement means focusing on who your child is, how they best receive love, what they need for their age and stage, and what they need in the moment.

God made every child unique. There is no guidebook for parenting, only helpful (and unhelpful) suggestions. Part of brokenness is that we don't have all the answers, and our ability to tune in and read our child's needs is imperfect. Many parents feel as though they are on survival mode, even with a tool belt full of resources and generations of love and care in their arsenal, let alone any parent without those resources and without that history of affection trying to pass the very best of attachment and attunement on to their child.

Brokenness will impact our childhoods and the childhoods of our children. But hope reminds us that, while early attachments are important, healing can happen in the parent/child relationship throughout our whole lives and their whole lives. Our parents and those closest to us will never be perfect. They will come with backstories of brokenness. Sin will wreak havoc, but God brings hope. No matter what our earliest days and years looked like, Jesus heals. He heals really, really messy things, and He heals things that seem only a little messy. Jesus makes a difference in everything. When we look at complicated childhoods, or complex attachments, we don't do so alone; Christ walks alongside us.

When I returned to therapy last autumn and asked for help for my unknown sadness and wrestling, I realized I was scared as I launched my daughter into the world, because launching had been hard for me. I wondered if after she left she would ever want to come back and play cards with me, tell her stories to me, or share her tears with me. The changes in our attachments as children grow are good. We can know they are good and still find them challenging.

Attachment gives us a sense of safety, a sense that we will be cared for and loved when the world presents its darker side. Later attachments can heal what was not present for us in our earlier attachments.[10] And Jesus can heal any relationship. Sometimes He does this during our lifetime here on earth; other times, we won't see healing until He comes again to restore all things.

God also redefines family through Jesus Christ. We create our own families and other intimate relationships as we grow. We see God valuing family in the New Testament, but God redefines family with Jesus' incarnation, sacrifice, resurrection, and ascension. We aren't dependent on a limited cultural lens of who we call family. There has always been a place for the sojourner in the midst of God's families throughout the Bible. Adoption and unexpected attachments were always part of the picture, but Jesus widens the picture further to bring more hope and more healing. In Mark 3:34–35, Jesus teaches His disciples to look for hope and healing, to provide hope and healing from the mess of family, in the Body of Christ: "And looking about at those who sat around Him, He said, 'Here are My mother and My brothers! For whoever does the will of God, he is My brother and sister and mother.'"

The Church is another place where we build attachments as we grow and one that helps heal attachments and relationships throughout our lifetime. We rely on more than our biological family for what we need. As Ephesians 3:14–19 teaches, Christ roots and grounds us in His love. God brings all kinds of new relationships into our lives throughout our life span. Our childhood struggles might be healed in a loving relationship with a friend, a mentor, or a spouse. Yet, any healing truly comes by Christ's love and in our relationship with Him.

When we look open-eyed at our experiences in our childhood and with our family of origin, we can more clearly see what we need from our current relationships. We gain new building blocks of intimacy. Those blocks build houses of healing for us and for the friends who gather there and for the next generation that grows there. I appreciate the way the late trauma clinician and researcher Dr. Francine Shapiro describes peering into our childhoods honestly to get to healing: "There is no blame here, only information."[11] Calling brokenness by name does not mean we are inviting in shame or blame; we are looking closer at it to see Hope more clearly.

No childhood is perfect. In the United States, we have a sense of nostalgia about childhood that isn't helping us heal or build stronger families now or in the future. The problem with nostalgia is that it sees only half the picture. God sees the good with the bad, the light with the dark. God sees the whole picture, including the brokenness of all families.

This is hope: families are always complicated, but the grace of Christ wraps around our lives in His cross and resurrection. God grows us, using our unique struggles and our unique families. He heals our pasts where they need healing and has plans and purposes for us at every age and stage. Christ is the foundation of healing in the midst of all the brokenness. Christ gives us a lens of grace and forgiveness to view our experiences in childhood and to help us build our own homes as adults.

With the support of our Redeemer who sets us free, we let go of the idealistic version of childhood and instead recognize the brokenness of every childhood while still honoring the joys and delight God intended for children as they grow. Each one of us grew up in a broken world. We are free from the expectations of painting a picture-perfect version of our family of origin, as well as the expectations to create a picture-perfect present. God does His restoration work by weaving hope into our stories.

ROMANTIC RELATIONSHIPS

romance

1 actions or relationships characterized by love and affection

There is a time in the developmental processes of growth when we all become adults. Just as Scripture says, there is "a time to be born, and a time to die . . . a time to weep, and a time to laugh . . . a time to keep, and a time to cast away" (Ecclesiastes 3:2, 4, 6). There is a time to be a child and a time to be an adult . . . a time to be dependent and a time to be independent . . . a time to eat from your mama's refrigerator and a time to eat from your own. As we grow older, our relationships change too; we grow into a greater capacity for reciprocal intimacy. Greater intimacy often means more complication in our relationships. This is true for all our relationships, and we'll discuss intimate friendships and community relationships in the next section. For now, we'll focus on the impact of brokenness in romantic relationships, particularly marriage, as adults.

In response to Adam and Eve's sin, which brought brokenness to the whole world, God issued a curse to Eve and Adam each independently (Genesis 3). This curse has a unique impact on us as we grow into adulthood and adult relationships:

> To the woman He said, "I will surely multiply your
> pain in childbearing; in pain you shall bring forth chil-
> dren. Your desire shall be contrary to [or toward] your
> husband,[12] but he shall rule over you." And to Adam He
> said, . . . "By the sweat of your face you shall eat bread,
> till you return to the ground, for out of it you were
> taken; for you are dust, and to dust you shall return."
> (Genesis 3:16–17, 19)

You don't need to see the latest romantic comedy to have a heartbeat on the tension within relationships between men and women. In the confusing language of both *contrary* and *toward* in Genesis 3:16, God introduces to women the push and pull they will feel in wanting protection and deep intimacy and also independence from men, which greatly impacts our experiences in marriage, the way we experience any romantic relationships, and our relationship with men in general. Men, on the other hand, have been given a different challenge in brokenness. God tells Adam he will have to work, and I don't think that work is limited to the ground and the provision of food. I think the curse's burden of work is felt in any vocation, and that includes relationships—husband, parent, neighbor, friend.

Perhaps you can see where men and women experience the consequences of both their own curse and the other's curse. When I walk a couple through premarriage or marriage counseling, the desire for both deep intimacy and independence is felt by both parties, but seems strongest for women. The desire to escape the work that relationships bring into our lives is also present for both parties, but seems strongest for men. This may be a reality. Yet men and women are likely to feel elements of the other's unique curse because sin and brokenness don't have neat boundaries.

The more I read Genesis 3, the more I have come to consider that the curse spoken by God over humankind is as much about Him identifying for us what He sees and knows will be the consequences of brokenness in our lives as it is about discipline. Christ heals the effects of brokenness in our life. While people who don't know Jesus' salvation might experience the benefit of healthy relationships, having a relationship with Christ greatly affects the presence of both forgiveness and freedom in our lives.

Because we have hormones and romantic interests from the teen years and beyond, and because marriage is only one relational vocation between men and women, I also think the weight of these curses will show up in our lives plenty, in and outside of marriage. God sees more to us than our relationship status. As people, I think sometimes we have a hard time doing the same. Singleness is in no way less of a life, and not all single people are seeking romantic intimacy or marriage intimacy. We bring one another relational safety when we offer grace-filled spaces to work out the place of romantic intimacy in each of our unique lives and when we avoid making assumptions about the place of romantic intimacy in anyone's life.

All of that said, marriage is a *uniquely* intimate relationship among adults, even while it is not a *superior* intimate relationship. I'd like to give the unique relationship of marriage some space here not only for those who are married, but with the recognition that all of us are impacted by marriage as we support one another in relationship.

According to Ephesians 5, marriage, any marriage, whether the couple is cognizant of it or not, reflects the relationship of

Christ and the Church. This passage also tells us that marriage's reflection of Christ and His Bride and this element of the interaction of husbands and wives is a great mystery, a mega mystery.[13]

One part of this mega mystery is that husbands and wives are separate parts but also a complete whole. Each member of the marriage exists fully integrated as "one flesh" while maintaining their uniqueness as individuals with different personalities, different wills, and different perspectives. One flesh is a biblical idea that holds some mystery. We see it first used in Genesis 2:24 and then by Jesus in the Gospel accounts of Matthew and Mark when talking about marriage. One flesh as we know it on earth is the wholeness of two persons in marriage while remaining separate. The tension of this intimacy and independence becomes especially clear in three areas of marriage: leaving and cleaving, the work of marriage, and the storms of marriage.

Leaving and cleaving is perhaps one of the most overlooked aspects of marriage. Maybe we rely too heavily on the mystery element of the one-flesh relationship and expect the leaving and cleaving to happen on its own. On the other hand, maybe we don't lean on the mystery enough, ignoring God's work in creating something new between two people.

We use the common defense mechanism called minimizing when we are confronted with change in life. We think that if we convince ourselves the change is only minimal, then we are protecting ourselves from the weight of that change in our lives. The changes that present themselves with marriage are rarely minimal. Marriage changes or intensifies the dynamics of a relationship, our awareness of the personalities within the relationship, and the weight of the consequences (and growth) from the relationship.

We live with the reality of brokenness pressed up against everything, especially those things that are most intimate to us— family, friends, faith. It is hard for parents when their children leave the nest, and while it is often lovely to invite a new son- or daughter-in-law into the fold, no relationship is instantly easy or without tension and transition. Sometimes the tension and transitional pain revolve more around the leaving, which all families experience in launching their young adults. Other times the tension and transitional pains revolve around the cleaving, or starting a new life as a family of two.

Leaving and cleaving is relational work that is done throughout adulthood and throughout marriage: Where are holidays spent? What information and decisions of adulthood do we share with our parents? How are our spouse and the people we are most intimate with different from what we knew growing up? This work is challenging for single individuals growing into their own lives, a couple navigating their new life, and parents and family members experiencing the leaving. It can also be joyful and exciting and a taste of adventure. We can wade through the broken aspects of leaving and cleaving better by giving time and attention to the needs and emotions that rise up among each individual involved, speaking to one another with truth, kindness, and compassion. When someone we care about takes vows in marriage, God asks us to change and grow also to make room for this new relationship the marriage has introduced.

Adulthood and marriage require work throughout the seasons of our lives. Some aspects of romantic relationships seem to pop up and remind us of the curse of brokenness again and again—the chores that never seem to be done, the inflexibility we find in ourselves and the one we love, the constant need for more growth and learning. Hope in Jesus reminds us that the work of any relationship is good work. Our sinful and selfish selves may want easy, but God gives us something better—deeper intimacy and the daily experience of both our need for forgiveness and God's willingness to give it.

Hope in Jesus reminds us that the work of any relationship is good work.

The hardest seasons of life and marriage are the storms. We want life, and especially love and marriage, to be a picture-perfect painting of us in a rowboat with strawberries and champagne or whiskey and sandwiches. Particularly in marriage, the squalls of life and our own brokenness make us want to turn away from each other. This turning away doesn't happen only in the big stuff, the lightning flashes; it also happens in tiny moments every day. We ignore our spouse for a TV show, we answer with a snip rather than a question, or we leave the trash in the bin a little longer than necessary to let them know we aren't controlled by their requests.

When someone asked Jesus about divorce, He repeated the Genesis account of the creation of marriage, including all the leaving and cleaving, and added only one sentence to the end. It's an informative addition:

> "Therefore a man shall leave his father and mother and hold fast to his wife, and the two shall become one flesh." So they are no longer two but one flesh. What therefore God has joined together, let not man separate. (Mark 10:7–9)

Jesus speaks here to the members of a marriage, asking them to turn toward each other rather than toward division.[14] Jesus was acquainted with the brokenness of this world as a living and breathing human being. He knew the risks. He knew the struggle. He remained without sin, but He knew the temptation to move toward separateness when brokenness pressed in. In our marriages, He asks us to lean in closer, to hold tightly to each other and to Him. Relationship research backs this up as well. Research from the Gottman Institute shows that "a tendency to turn toward your partner is the basis of trust, emotional connection, passion, and a satisfying sex life."[15]

Turning toward isn't limited to marriage, however. How often are we tempted toward separateness when confronted with struggle in any relationship? Boundaries have their place, but the question is worth considering. In adulthood, we begin to confront the storms brokenness brings into our lives. There will be big storms and littler storms and monstrous storms. When the storms come, we often want to turn away from our relationships, including our marriages. In these storms, we think we are saving ourselves some pain by turning away, but what we are really doing is letting go of the anchor.

Divorce is one aspect of brokenness in this world. Many, if not all, of us have been touched by divorce. This aspect of brokenness is not outside of Jesus' healing. The challenge is to seek God's wisdom before our own, to call out the brokenness and see His hope in our lives. There are marriages and relationships in this life that will need to be broken. In our brokenness, sorting through the need for divorce or another relationship cutoff is never without our sin and also is never *only* about our sin. There is "a time to tear, and a time to sew; a time to keep silence, and a time to speak," according to Ecclesiastes 3:7. Relationships in a broken world will hold the full host of these things. If you are wrestling with or have wrestled with divorce for your marriage, the best advice I have is to turn toward the Savior and His Word to help sort out all the chaos and gunk. He holds the answer for each of our situations in their complexities and nuances. He is both perfect love and perfect justice, when we have a limited view of both.

The brokenness of divorce is sometimes about issues of betrayal and safety. Other times, however, couples experience feeling stuck in a cycle of the hard and broken things of this life. When we turn toward the people in our lives, especially our spouses, Jesus often gives us a concrete reminder that His hope is an anchor in our lives. Spouses aren't Jesus. Jesus wouldn't leave coffee cups on the counter when the dishwasher is right there, and He wouldn't ever say hurtful things. When our spouse shows us our imperfections, we get a glimpse into our need for something more, *someone more* to hold onto us, to keep our boat from capsizing. When our spouse fails us or can't protect us from the brokenness of the world, Jesus is more for us than any romantic relationship can offer:

> We have this as a sure and steadfast anchor of the soul, a hope that enters into the inner place behind the curtain, where Jesus has gone as a forerunner on our behalf, having become a high priest forever after the order of Melchizedek. (Hebrews 6:19–20)

Life and relationships hold lots of good stuff, but man, when the bad stuff comes, it seems incessant. The broken things of life and relationships can be disorienting, like sheets of rain. They make it hard to see the anchor and one another. But this is hope: Jesus turns toward us always. He brings hope in the moments when those storms pummel and overwhelm. In hope, we hold fast to Jesus, our anchor, as we navigate the world of adulthood and all its relationships, including the romantic ones.

FAMILY LIFE

family

1 a group of individuals who share a common ancestry

2 a group of individuals who offer care and a sense of protection
   to one another, as well as a stated commitment toward one
   another, legal or otherwise, which creates a unique bond and
   responsibility that goes beyond friendship

Family and *home* can be the best words of life for some, while
for others these words might bring more pain. Most of us land
somewhere in the middle, holding both the comfort and the challenges of family close to our chests. Every family has their quirks,
traditions, histories, challenges, and trials. Each of us are left
with something to unpack related to our family.

For me, the unpacking began with the term "blended family," introduced to me in a ministry to the family course I took
in college at age 19. Before that course, I didn't have words for
the combination of happiness, pain, and scrappiness that was my
family. Other families seemed to me like a garment cut out with
a pattern and sewn together perfectly. My family was more like
a flannel jacket with various patches sewn together imperfectly, but full of comfort and character. As a teenager, I wanted my

family to be less threadbare and mismatched, more "normal." The idea that families are often "blended" also introduced me to a surprisingly comforting reality: broken is normal. We cannot produce perfect families in a broken world. Each family will have their mess and their heartbreak alongside their triumphs and strengths. In this way, whatever picture of "normal" we have in our head hasn't existed since the Garden of Eden. When we are honest about the brokenness in every family and help them call their own breed of brokenness by name, we stop striving for normal and can more easily find hope in the midst of the brokenness. Hope is found in many small and large ways amid family life, from encouraging conversations to simply knowing you have a place to land, however broken it may be. Yet we often need Jesus-sized hope in family life, because without Jesus, we can't get to grace, forgiveness, and true restoration. The hope of Jesus—seated in the restorative power of His death and resurrection and general investment in our lives—changes the shape of imperfection and brokenness in the intimate places of our lives, which then overflows into every area.

Perfection doesn't need grace. In that way, grace audaciously identifies brokenness in order to bring about restoration. Grace is about second chances, and second chances bring us hope. The grace of forgiveness and re-creation found in Jesus Christ is for families in the same way it is available for us as individuals. Much of family life happens in close proximity to one another. There is a depth of intimacy in families that lays bare to one another in technicolor our individual brokenness and imperfections. There is also hope in knowing that growth happens, both in us as individuals and in our families, when the truth of our flaws and our sin is out in the open. Jesus shines light in our darkest moments and also in the mundane ones: an argument that moves us to apologies, an opportunity to learn kindness and emotional skills, encouragement to advocate for what we need.

Family life is broken people living together, sharing hope.

Family life is broken people living together, sharing hope.

I used to think it was the job of my family to help me escape the brokenness of the world. But we will never, not one of us, escape brokenness. When avoiding brokenness is the goal, we heap unrealistic expectations on ourselves and our families to be something that is only possible in the ever after, in the time when Jesus comes again. That will be a glorious day, but it isn't our day now. Stuffing the struggles of family life down to *appear* less broken brings a sense of stigma and shame within our families. We are seeing the unfortunate impact of this stigma on society as a whole—failure to get help when we need it, more feelings of isolation than ever, and more anxiety within the family system and systems they interact with, such as schools and churches.[16]

Hope can be found more clearly in the day-to-day of family life by actively confessing our sins and struggles out loud, acknowledging the challenges and areas where we carry guilt. When our confession is received with grace in the intimacy of family life, children and adults alike see and experience Jesus' presence in the room, which is another kind of hope in our lives. Jesus' grace then points us toward growth, another powerful expression of hope.

No family's breed of brokenness is outside the hands of God the Father. Acknowledging brokenness in our families, without excusing anyone's part in it, allows us to see hope in the middle of some of the most important and complex relationships in our lives. Ephesians 3:14–19 reminds us that the strong roots of a family are not perfect relationships or even healthy ones, but God the Father's love and mercy:

> For this reason I bow my knees before the Father, from whom every family in heaven and on earth is named, that according to the riches of His glory He may grant you to be strengthened with power through His Spirit in your inner being, so that Christ may dwell in your hearts through faith—that you, being rooted and grounded in love, may have strength to comprehend with all the saints what is the breadth and length and height and depth, and to know the love of Christ that surpasses knowledge, that you may be filled with all the fullness of God.

Understanding the breadth and length and height and depth of Christ's love that doesn't require something from us is the heart of family life and family health. Sociological research also reveals that families who report sharing spiritual values, affection, and a strong sense of togetherness also report a higher sense of thriving as a family.[17] This is no mistake. This is hope living in those families. Knowing Christ's love comes through hearing and being taught the Word of God, but we *understand* Christ's love for us as individuals when we also experience it in our lives alongside the knowledge.

As we work and talk and play and grow in our families, Law and Gospel, sin and forgiveness, brokenness and hope make more sense; they seem tangible instead of being faraway ideas. To understand the interaction of these more tangible areas of brokenness and grace in family life, we turn to two spiritual purposes of family life that greatly affect our emotional, vocational, and relational lives, both as children and adults: safety and knowing. Safety is the sense of attachment in our lives; a sense of tethering in the storm; a sense that, come what may, our relationships will remain intact and we won't be left in this world on our own. Knowing is a deep sense that we are both deeply connected to others and unique as individuals in this world. It is both identity and belonging wrapped into a concoction in our souls that reminds us we matter, to people and to God.

Why are safety and knowing so important in family life? The Book of Ephesians gives us some clues. In Ephesians, Paul has a lot to say about all kinds of relationships, but he especially dedicates a lot of space to two specific relationships: the ones we call family (by genetics or adoption) and those within the Body of Christ, which is identified throughout the New Testament as a family for us. Once the Body of Christ is created by God with the arrival of the Holy Spirit, we immediately see the family and the church family working side by side in many vocational roles culturally expected of the immediate family structure—such as caring for widows, teaching people of all ages, and sharing food in communal meals. The New Testament offers plenty of counsel for taking care of our families by birth, marriage, and adoption. Yet God also expands the way we think of family into this Body He has created called the Church. Because of this overlap, passages in Scripture that speak about the Church are applicable to family life, and passages that speak of family life are applicable within the Church. We'll look more into the place of the Body of Christ in our lives in the next section; for now, let's stay with how safety and knowing are instrumental in our immediate family life.

Ephesians 4:15–16 reminds us that the way we use language can connect and build up family members in love, priming each individual for growth:

> Rather, speaking the truth in love, we are to grow up in every way into Him who is the head, into Christ, from whom the whole body, joined and held together by every joint with which it is equipped, when each part is working properly, makes the body grow so that it builds itself up in love.

God is love, and we understand God through the Word He gives us. When we read and share Scripture in our families, we hear who God tells us we are, giving us a better understanding of our identity in this world with its many confusing messages about identity. When we hear and discuss God's restorative grace in the middle of brokenness—which is all over the accounts in the Bible—we have a sense that grace is available in our broken lives too. Even parents, spouses, and siblings who love us will mess up. When we use words of God's grace to heal and repair those moments and relationships in love, we feel a sense of safety. This immediate sense of safety, especially when we are children, also helps us to have a stronger sense of the unchanging safety of God's love.

Perfect parents, perfect spouses, perfect family members do not exist in this broken world. Forgiven and loved family members do. As humans, we perceive hope in both God's words and actions in the Bible, but we understand that hope through the people in our lives, our most intimate relationships, as they speak and act in truth and love. These experiences of perceiving hope in our day-to-day lives help the truth and love of God to show up like bold print in our hearts and minds.

In our relationships, truth and love often translate to boundaries and affection. Because we are broken people, we are tempted to swing toward one or the other—truth over love or love over truth. Ephesians reminds us to speak truth *in* love to promote growth. For example, we can offer affection physically by hugs and comfort, intellectually by listening to interests and ideas, and emotionally by opening conversations of all kinds about the good things of life and the hard things of life. We set boundaries by having rules, but also flexibility. We create a sense of safety when we have rules with flexibility and discuss them openly with authority and accountability, but also with affection.

Because God offers freedom in Christ, we can offer freedom in our families as well: freedom to fail, freedom to be forgiven when we fail, freedom to figure life out with some support.

A foundational verse for families, and for any relationship, is Galatians 5:1: "For freedom Christ has set us free; stand firm therefore, and do not submit again to a yoke of slavery." Wrestling with truth and love means wrestling with freedom. What does Christ's freedom look like in families? I think most of the time it means room for mistakes. God allowed space in this world for humankind's mistakes, even though He knew it would bring brokenness. God also provided His Son to redeem our brokenness and to bring us hope. Because God offers freedom in Christ, we can offer freedom in our families as well: freedom to fail, freedom to be forgiven when we fail, freedom to figure life out with some support.

Another way we build safety and knowing in our relationships is through the biblical concept of honor. Honor is no small word. The idea of honor is connected to sacrifice, as in military honor, but also to kindness and expressing value. Think of a small child holding out a dandelion for his or her mother. It's a gift that says, "I thought of you, and this is a small way I can show you that you matter in my life." God shows us that He honors us by sending Jesus into our brokenness. We don't deserve this honor, but God bestows it anyway: "Because you are precious in My eyes, and honored, and I love you, I give men in return for you, peoples in exchange for your life" (Isaiah 43:4). Neither should the honor we give to our family members be dependent on their goodness or their have-it-together-ness. Bestowing honor, showing one another we each have value even in our mistakes and brokenness, gives us a sense of safety and intimacy.

Bestowing honor in a family can look like many things, and I encourage you to consider where you see it or don't see it in your own family life. Here are just some of the ways we can show honor in family life:

- speaking in kindness, even when we discipline or disagree
- holding one another accountable while also extending grace
- listening to understand

- treating one another with respect in words and actions, without name-calling or put-downs

- building trust by sharing time together and sharing stories, experiences, likes, and dislikes

- sharing ideas with one another and allowing for creativity

- empathizing when life is hard or we are hurt

Forgiveness, freedom, truth and love, honor—each of these biblical ideas builds safety and intimacy in our homes and within our family units. They aren't a solution to brokenness, but they do allow us to see hope in the middle of the brokenness of our lives and particularly in our family life.

This is hope: there is no road without its obstacles in family life, no map for family life. But each road we find ourselves on, God is there too. He walks, drives, bikes, and jogs alongside us. We might be looking for the one right system for how to do family life, the perfect route, the way to finally get to the pretend destination of "normal." Instead, God gives us hope.

God loves families. God loves your family. We can't do this thing called family life without Him. But in Jesus, we find an intimacy and safety in family life that grows us. Christ's forgiveness, boundaries, and affection in our family life leave a trail of hope in the very "normal" brokenness.

MESSES IN COMMUNITY: BROKEN BELONGING

connection

1 the sensation or state of being joined with someone or something, rather than only alone

community

1 often understood as a place where people share some kind of commonality

2 the places and people we call home during our time here on earth

3 supportive relationships developed intentionally by a group of individuals that includes regular connection and honest participation in life together, which produces a sense of belonging

Community is a word that gets tossed around a lot. When we picture a community, I think we mostly picture buildings, roads, grocery stores, and schools. We also might picture the vocations of people who serve in our communities—postal workers, nurses, teachers, firefighters, restaurant workers, and more. And often our view of community is limited to what we know and have experienced, which means our picture of community is often limited to people who look and think like us.

During my therapy sessions, the idea of community came up a lot. I found I was wrestling with my place in the various communities of my life—geographic, cultural, and spiritual. I needed a supportive space to do this wrestling out loud. The concept of community was like a weight pressing onto my chest. I wanted more from the relationships I had found outside of my immediate family. I struggled with the impact of brokenness on my experience of community. Brokenness was alive in my friendships, my church, and my neighborhood, just as it was in me and in my family.

In conversations with my own therapy clients or others I connect with, I often hear a longing for a deeper sense of community, of genuineness in community. Many of us long for a sense of genuine community. It seems evident to me that many of us want life together, not life sort of living close by one another. Brokenness, however, complicates our ability to create relationships, maintain relationships, and discern healthy community. To get to the heart of genuineness in community, we start by unraveling the concept of connection. We need connection. We were created for connection. God wants to be connected to us and wants us to be connected to one another.

Connection is the invisible work of God in our lives. According to Colossians 1:16–17, He is the mighty connector: "For by Him all things were created, in heaven and on earth, visible and invisible, whether thrones or dominions or rulers or authorities—all things were created through Him and for Him. And He is before all things, and in Him all things hold together." God the Father, Son, and Spirit lived in Trinity long before our arrival here. They are the first and greatest connection, and God in Trinity holds all other connections together.

When brokenness calls, "You are alone," hope and community call, "Not in Christ."

Connection isn't everything though; it's not the end goal. It's a lovely step toward community. Momentary connections build on one another toward something more. Connections bring us a sense of awareness that we aren't alone in the world, but community brings us a shared sense of belonging. This sense of belonging transforms our internal thoughts and feelings of connection into actions and behaviors that create what author and activist Dietrich Bonhoeffer called life together. Life together is genuine community that shares a common purpose and meets one another's needs. Connection removes, for a moment, the sense of isolation that brokenness brings into our lives. Community and life together remove the sense of isolation for the long haul.

When brokenness calls, "You are alone," hope and community call, "Not in Christ."

CONNECTION AND BELONGING

belonging

1 holding membership or entitlement within an organization or group

2 a sense that we are in this together; that you are not alone; that in your hour of need or joy, your people will show up for you, and you will show up for them in theirs

Brokenness, by nature, is disconnection. Brokenness "broke" our relationship with God and the people all around us. It severed and continues to sever connections. We naturally seek reconnection. We have an internal sense that we were not made to go this life alone, but Satan and the mess of brokenness in this world make it less clear how we are to go about reconnecting or what healthy reconnection looks like. God sent Jesus Christ so that our connection to Him could be restored by grace and so we could be included in the community that is Christ and His Body. Christ is the ultimate provider of a sense of belonging to our broken internal system, shattered by our own sin and the sin and yuck of the world.

With a healed connection between the world and God in Christ, we can move in this world, creating and maintaining healthy connections with people all around us. Brokenness will still be present and a part of every connection and every community. Some will not know Christ. Those of us who know Christ will not fully understand the health and healing Christ brings. We will hurt and be hurt. We will wrestle with health in relationships until Jesus comes again with perfect health. The hope of Christ brings meaning to the struggles of our communities.

The Law is useful for relationships—do this, don't do that—but Christ's Gospel brings hope into relationships that the Law cannot, which is one reason we'll experience relationships differently inside the Body of Christ than outside of it. Yet God does care about all friendships, our towns and our neighborhoods, our schools and other places of relationship in our lives. God's salvation is found in Jesus, but God's grace is not limited to Jesus. He connects us and creates community as what we call a First Article gift, referring to the first segment of the Apostles' Creed, "I believe in God, the Father Almighty, Maker of heaven and earth." As Father of all things, God has a heart for all things. People are allowed to say, "No, thank You," to Jesus and eternity and still reap at least partial benefits of God's gifts of connection, belonging, and community during their short time on this planet.

As Christians, we enter into every relationship *in Christ*, even when we connect and grow alongside unbelievers. Because our belonging is secure in Christ, we can create connections without asking the people we're connecting with to bear the full weight of helping us feel like we belong. There is hope in the security of our relationship with the God of the universe. This hope feeds our other relationships. When feelings of lack or a sense that we don't fit or aren't enough well up, we always have Someone to turn to.

And God faithfully builds belonging in our earthly relationships as part of His grace, even when that belonging is imperfect. Deeper than the momentary spark of connection among people, belonging is built by those connections growing deeper over time. Suffering and rejoicing together are the biblical hallmarks of the extended connectedness that leads to belonging and true community: "If one member suffers, all suffer together; if one member is honored, all rejoice together. Now you are the body of Christ and individually members of it" (1 Corinthians 12:26–27). This passage describes God's design for life together in the Body of Christ. Humanity is hungry for connectedness and community with one another. The people of God coming together in community is God's answer for sharing the fullness of the Gospel in our world and communities.

Humanity is hungry for connectedness and community with one another.

It's so easy to think we can build community by relying on the *bonuses* of grace though—the soccer games and schools, the committees and neighborhoods. But they are just that: a bonus. They might add to our sense of belonging, but they cannot be a substitute for the belonging we have in Jesus and the internal awareness of belonging that comes with bearing our burdens together, sharing hope, and cheering for one another's victories.

We can build on the foundational belonging that God gives us in Christ by digging deeper into connecting in intimacy with those around us and building community over time. Remember, all humans long for deep intimacy, and in sharing intimacy we also make the path clearer for sharing the Gospel in a way people can hear it. People all around us are lonely. Maybe you are experiencing loneliness. Loneliness, like its cousin brokenness, comes in all shapes and sizes. In his book *Together*, Vivek H. Murthy, a doctor and former Surgeon General of the United States, identifies from research three layers of loneliness people experience: [18]

- Emotional—the sense of an absence of a heart and soul connection that helps us feel like we matter or would be missed in our absence

- Social—the sense of an absence of a mind and heart connection that comes with social relationships and companionships of differing depths

- Collective—the absence of a sense of belonging to a bigger community

And yet this is hope: we might experience loneliness, but we don't have to go this broken life alone. God places us in specific times and places. Connection meets loneliness wherever we are. God gives us this gift of connection to begin the process and Himself sustains the process of community—maybe it's a conversation at the back of the church, a hello to a neighbor, or a shared cause with someone across the globe. Some of these relationships deepen into friendships with many connections, organically or intentionally. We start to share more about ourselves and receive more from someone else. We begin to suffer and rejoice in genuine life together.

We want people in our lives to laugh with but also to cry with. We want people to share dinner with and also to ask us how we *really* are when we say, "Fine." Connection can certainly include having fun together and shared interests, but community is so much more. The belonging that community brings creates relationships that don't turn away from our brokenness, relationships that meet us in our brand of loneliness. Jesus' restoration is coming. In that day, we will have the truest sense of connection and community and belonging in us and all around us every day with God and one another. In the meantime, look around you. What connections is He making in your life today? What community is He inviting you to grow?

FRIENDSHIP

friendship

1 a mutual state of affection, support, trust, and honor

2 a relationship that is exceptional in its closeness, outside the norm of occasional and coincidental human connection

Whether you are young or old, male or female, you were made for friendship. It is valuable for your mental and physical health.[19] It also takes far more effort than we usually care to admit. When C. S. Lewis wrote about friendship in *The Four Loves*, he wrote about every human's innate desire for friendship, the sacrifices required for friendship, and the process of friendship. Unfortunately, what he is famously quoted for is only a single aspect of friendship, which is connection.

What we think Lewis said: Friendship is "What? You too? I thought I was the only one."

What Lewis actually said: "The typical expression of opening Friendship would be something like, 'What? You too? I thought I was the only one.'"[20]

Friendships *start* with openings. Friendships continue by growing in intimacy.

Some friendships endure in this process for a lifetime, others for a season, and still others a moment. Some fade like the sunset, and some end abruptly in fireworks. We talk of friendship as though it is something that merely exists, but like all relationships, it requires work. The work of relationship is part of the consequences of brokenness from Genesis 3. We are made to be in relationship with God and one another, but those relationships were ruptured when brokenness entered the world. That rupture includes all of our "one anothers"—family, friendship, life in the church, our groups and clubs, our communities, and the world at large.

We could talk all day long about friendship and never scratch the surface, but in this chapter, I want to give a brief overview of what the Bible has to say about friendship in order to gain some understanding of the role of friendship in our lives.

We were always intended to experience perfect love and affection from God first and foremost. This includes *agape*, or unconditional love, but it also includes friendship. Our very first friend available to us from before we were born is God. Christ's sacrifice cements our ability to live in friendship with God. It is our reality in Christ, when friendship with people can seem like a far-off wish or desire. Christ came to make friendship between God and humans possible, which demonstrates to us how greatly God values friendship with His people.

We will always be safest, and best known, by God. Our broken relationship with God from our sin and sin's existence in the world is repaired through the death and resurrection of Jesus Christ. Our relationship with Christ is irreplaceable for many reasons, salvation being chief among them. In John 15, Jesus talks about His relationship with us as Savior, which enables us to connect with Him as friend. What a privilege it is to be considered not only child, not only sibling, but also *friend* by the God of the universe!

John 15:9–15 reveals some nuts and bolts about friendship:

> As the Father has loved Me, so have I loved you. Abide in My love. If you keep My commandments, you will abide in My love, just as I have kept My Father's commandments and abide in His love. These things I have spoken to you, that My joy may be in you, and that your joy may be full. This is My commandment, that you love one another as I have loved you. Greater love has no one than this, that someone lay down his life for his friends. You are My friends if you do what I command you. No longer do I call you servants, for the servant does not know what his master is doing; but I have called you friends, for all that I have heard from My Father I have made known to you.

Jesus abides with us. He came down to this broken world and taught people. He ate supper and traveled and cried with the people all around Him. He sought people out. He came to earth with the express purpose of sacrificing His life for those people and for *all* people, so that we could be called friend by Him. He continues to abide with us in His Spirit and His Word.

This term *abiding* is a massive piece to the friendship puzzle. There is no friendship where there is no connection, and no friendship can be sustained without abiding. This is true for our friendship with Jesus and with other people. Friendships begin because someone showed up initially, because someone connected initially. But friendships continue because they connected again and again. My friendship with Jesus is based solely on the reality that He showed up for me, He sacrificed for me, and He continues to show up for me, abiding with me. These three pieces—showing up, sacrificing, and abiding—are elemental to any authentic friendship.

These three pieces—showing up, sacrificing, and abiding—are elemental to any authentic friendship.

God is the provider of all our needs—of food, water, shelter, but also much more. He gives us friends as another of His provisions. Sometimes in the brokenness of life, the curse of the work of relationship can make it feel as though we have no friends or have no faithful friends. God is never unfaithful in providing for us, but friendship can be one of the most challenging relational areas for many people. Because brokenness leaves its impact on finding, and keeping, friendships, we will often need to lean into our first friend, Jesus, for hope in this particular struggle as well. But friendship is worth the effort: a robust conversation is healthy for our minds; someone to listen and advise is good for our hearts; and people in the "great cloud" become real to our souls in individual relationships.

How do we make and keep solid friendships in a broken world? What do showing up, sacrificing, and abiding look like in real life?

We start by abiding in Jesus, which takes the weight of our need off of people and places it on Christ. Then, all friendships begin with a bid for connection. This is showing up level one. It requires vulnerability to reach out to a stranger and say, "Hi, my name is . . ." We cannot skip past this stage. We have to start somewhere.

In his book *The Relationship Cure*, relationship expert John Gottman defines a bid for connection as any question, look, gesture, or expression that communicates, "I want to feel connected to you."[21] Bids for connection continue throughout relationships, little moments of people showing up for one another time after time.

In brokenness, we do this bidding and connecting imperfectly. But Christ-followers are covered in Christ. We can be vulnerable and reach out in friendship because God was willing to be vulnerable with us. When we don't get invited to the party, when people fail to send the bids or reach out in friendship, it feels like middle school all over again—and no one wants to go back to middle school. There will be people we don't connect with, and that's okay, because our friendship with Christ really is enough. Everything else in this life is a bonus. God also gives us freedom in this life to say no to some friendships. When boundaries are necessary, He provides for us in this way too. We rest in Him, spend time in His Word, and then go out to connect in new and different ways.

In a strange twist, the awkwardness that comes with failed bids and bids left behind can actually work to deepen friendship as well—the sacrifice of forgiveness. In forgiveness, we sacrifice by confessing our mistakes and our brokenness to one another. In forgiveness, we sacrifice by offering the olive branch when we've been hurt. Together, the vulnerability of awkward moments and forgiveness can move us past the opening connection of friendship and on to growth. If we don't keep showing up for one another, even at our weirdest and our ugliest, then our connection will remain shallow, and that's not friendship. That's acquaintanceship.

An example might be helpful to see how friendship grows through bids for connection and forgiveness. Here's a little story I like to call "The Starbucks Card Debacle":

I met Tamara while speaking at a retreat for pastors' wives. I complimented her on her polka dot glasses and Star Wars shirt (bid). We talked more Star Wars (more bids), and so it began. Our acquaintanceship continued in a rather disconnected fashion via a Facebook group of fellow pastors' wives. We didn't know each other well, or at all, beyond our admiration of the empire that is George Lucas.

Then, one summer day, she posted in the Facebook group that she was looking for hotel recommendations for a conference her husband was attending somewhat near my house. I fired off a response: "You and the kids should come stay at our house! We'll feed you. I have wine" (more bidding). Instead of replying back, "Hey, Weirdo-I-Hardly-Know, thanks but no thanks," Tamara responded, "Hmmm, that might work! I'll private message you to figure it out."

Tamara came. Our kids played dress-up and sidewalk chalked the entire driveway. They fed us fake food from their very legitimate fake restaurants. In the evenings, Tamara and I drank wine and ate chocolate and talked about life, motherhood, our gifts, and the struggles of finding the best place to use them (abiding).

This story of friendship gets truly interesting when our time together ended and Tamara and the kids went home. She sent me a lovely, entirely unnecessary thank-you note with a Starbucks gift card tucked inside. The debacle began when the gift card registered a zero-sum balance everywhere I tried to use it. I wrestled with whether to tell Tamara or just let it go. I ended up messaging her because I knew she had spent money from a stash of limited funds to supply this gift . . . and because I really like coffee.

When I messaged, I thanked her for her unnecessary gift and told her about the problem. I used lots of phrases like "no big deal" and "don't even worry about it" alongside "just wanted to let you know in case you can get your money back" (bid, mixed with confession).

Can you imagine the awkwardness of the situation? Tamara went back to the source of her gift card and made sure the balance was actually applied this time. I drank my coffee and messaged her back saying I was sorry for the inconvenience again, and her response will stay with me forever: "Nothing cements a friendship like awkward." Tamara also apologized profusely. I apologized profusely for the whole ordeal (forgiveness).

Forgiveness doesn't need to be necessary to be given. Because we were willing to be vulnerable for a moment and then another and another, we grew. We didn't know whether our vulnerability would be received each step of the way. We sat together and shared our experiences of brokenness in this life, and we experienced together some of the really weird ways the world is broken as a whole. We grew some more. When we celebrated the mutual care and forgiveness of even the unnecessary in Jesus, we grew together exponentially.

Tamara and I are still friends today because we share more than this Starbucks Card Debacle. Every relationship will be tested in the fire of brokenness in real life. People will hurt one another, even unintentionally. There will also be times when a friend is pummeled by semitrucks of brokenness crashing into his or her life. Will we continue to abide with one another in these dark times? The friendships that sit with us, check on us, and still continue eating at our tables when we have been stripped bare by hardship, these are the ones that remain while others crash or fade.

The brokenness of the world means that work and wild amounts of effort will be a part of every friendship our entire lives. We want finding friends to be easy. We want the bidding to come easily. We want to grow together easily. We want friendship without hiccups or heartaches and the subsequent forgiveness and sacrifice. In all these things, it feels like brokenness prevails.

Christ's hope burns brighter: We are never rejected by Christ, never outcast, never outside the circle of friends. We abide in Christ, and He fosters that abiding between us. Friendship brings hope into our lives as a continual reminder that we are not alone, connected both in the "Me toos!" of friendship and in sitting with one another in the broken places of this life.

THE BODY OF CHRIST

Body of Christ

1 the community of Christ-followers connected by God through His Word and the saving work of Jesus, as well as a life lived suffering and rejoicing together in His Spirit

2 the group of people called "the Church," when referring to the whole of God's people across time and space who have come to saving faith in Christ Jesus; and the group of people commonly called "the church" when referring to the local body of believers, often called a congregation

3 the bread served at Communion, which mysteriously connects the members of the Church on earth and in heaven

Often life looks more disheveled than we'd like. As I sit at my computer typing, the planet rotates as usual, but most things around me are not what we might call normal. There are masks and stay-at-home orders and cancellations and adjustments in response to a worldwide pandemic. We talk about it like it's a houseguest who has dropped in uninvited and overstayed its welcome—COVID, the annoying party crasher.

Until these last few months, I only knew the word *pandemic* as the title of a fun board game. This, unlike the game, is not fun. There have been some lovely moments of family time mixed into the monotony and challenges of working, schooling, meeting, and organizing all of life from home. Yet the larger chorus all around me is a sudden awareness of brokenness. COVID has reminded us that we aren't in control of everything, not everything is fixable, and there are things with no quick or easy answer.

I have noticed people around me realizing once again the basic human need for connection and community. These things, which we once deemed optional or afterthoughts, are given their place alongside other basic needs, such as nutrition or exercise. However, many of us have a hard time understanding what community and connection really are. We fill ourselves with what we think community is but come away empty rather than full. Appointments and events fill our schedules as we attempt to connect with others, but we often come up short, with little connection and more exhaustion.

God brought us the gift of the Church on earth to help fill this need for connection. Social distancing and stay-at-home orders remind us that the connection and community the Church brings into our lives are not limited to buildings with walls.

The Body of Christ is the people of God across time and space who have come to a saving faith in Jesus Christ, who believe in His sacrifice and resurrection. God could bring the message of Hope into the brokenness of this world any way He wants. Yet He gathers people around His tangible gifts—His Word, Baptism, forgiveness, the Lord's Supper—and uses those people to spread Hope.

Sometimes though, in our own sinfulness and in the confusion of brokenness all around us, we end up burying the Church like a treasure hidden in a field (Matthew 13:44–46). We tuck ourselves away, trying to keep ourselves from troubling things. We do this as a people of God, just as we do as individuals who follow God. Big questions of brokenness, such as suicide, domestic violence, mental illness, community violence, and racism, leave us wanting to disconnect, or stay within our walls and fences, instead of connecting to a world in need of Hope.

It's tempting as Christians to reserve the suffering and rejoicing of life together for relationships only within the Church. But these building blocks of relationship can also serve us when we try to connect the world to Jesus and His hope. We are never without God's Word wherever we go. And as temples of the Holy Spirit, we are never without God's presence either. We may struggle to perceive it, but He is faithful. Sometimes we would really love it if God's plans were to set us apart as the Church to stay *away* from this world and all its trouble and brokenness. According to Jesus' teaching in John 17:14–19, we are each meant to be in the world with the Word in our hands. We live in community with other believers in order to strengthen us to engage the wider geographic and relational communities we have been placed in by God Himself.

Within the Body of Christ, "community" is first a bestowed reality of God in Christ Jesus. God *calls* us a connected community in His Word. First Corinthians 12:14–20 is true whether we opt into the experience or not:

> For the body does not consist of one member but of
> many. If the foot should say, "Because I am not a hand,
> I do not belong to the body," that would not make it
> any less a part of the body. And if the ear should say,
> "Because I am not an eye, I do not belong to the body,"

that would not make it any less a part of the body. If
the whole body were an eye, where would be the sense
of hearing? If the whole body were an ear, where would
be the sense of smell? But as it is, God arranged the
members in the body, each one of them, as He chose.
If all were a single member, where would the body be?
As it is, there are many parts, yet one body.

Members of the Body of Christ are connected, each performing an invisible part. When we drive our cars, the engine and wheels and pistons and all the parts work regardless of whether we can see them or understand them. So it is with the Body of Christ. We are connected, forming a community. Period. End of sentence. In this way, God's Body is exceptional in this world, because it is not broken. The Holy Spirit protects it, sustains it, and gives it invisible strength.

However, connection and community are also things we work toward and grow into in the Body of Christ. First Thessalonians 5:11 uses the language of building and constructing to describe how community is developed within the Body: "Therefore encourage one another and build one another up, just as you are doing."

God's Church will always continue as a community, whether we are doing the work of encouraging and building one another up or not. But when we avoid that work or simply fail to address it, we will feel the weight of disconnection, the lack of authenticity in the community. Sometimes brokenness leaves us sluggish or uninvested, scared to invest, frankly, which leads to fewer moments of connection. Without moments of connection, our experience of community becomes torn. We move from actively suffering and rejoicing together in the Body to disconnection to divorcing ourselves from the community or living without a sense of belonging in the community.

There is hope in God's ability also to repair community bit by bit through moments of connection. In Christ Jesus' mercy, we will always be members of the Body of Christ, even when we are missing that sense of belonging, even when we have walked away from that community for a time. The visible communities we call churches are deeply impacted by the brokenness of this world, just as every other thing in this world is impacted by brokenness. Indeed, if we are embracing the depth of intimacy intended for the Body of Christ, relational brokenness will feel strikingly strong at times. Many places in Scripture use family themes to describe the Body of Christ. Family is where we tend to let all our baggage out, but it's also a place where that baggage can be wrestled with in safety and knowing. If the Body's members are sharing more of their brokenness, rather than hiding it, we will feel uncomfortable and sometimes more broken within the Body.

No matter where we encounter brokenness, the answer is the same: hope in Jesus Christ.

No matter where we encounter brokenness, the answer is the same: hope in Jesus Christ. His forgiveness and grace and kindness integrate us back together time and again—internally, in our families, in our friendships, and in this Body of Christ. Sometimes we assume grace and forgiveness just ooze out of the Body of Christ, but we have the opportunity to actively engage in sharing grace and forgiveness in our midst instead of waiting around for it to show itself. We speak this grace actively by sharing the Word of God with one another, by creating places to discuss what God's Word has to say about the joys and struggles of life. We have the opportunity to be fed by grace in the Lord's Supper. And we also share grace when we weep and laugh with one another in our church buildings and ministry centers, as well as outside of them.

The Body of Christ also builds a sense of belonging for people by helping every member see they have a place here. We don't need to hide our experiences of brokenness, though we can offer discretion and treat them with care. First Corinthians 12:21–27 teaches us that the Body of Christ actually brings honor when a member experiences something that seems unpresentable:

> The eye cannot say to the hand, "I have no need of you," nor again the head to the feet, "I have no need of you." On the contrary, the parts of the body that seem to be weaker are indispensable, and on those parts of the body that we think less honorable we bestow the greater honor, and our unpresentable parts are treated with greater modesty, which our more presentable parts do not require. But God has so composed the body, giving greater honor to the part that lacked it, that there may be no division in the body, but that the members may have the same care for one another. If one member suffers, all suffer together; if one member is honored, all rejoice together. Now you are the body of Christ and individually members of it.

This means that part of our work together in the Body of Christ is noticing one another. It is a gift to be seen in our suffering, to be honored as we experience brokenness in our lives. We will all hurt at one time or another and need some help. Your experiences of brokenness, your neighbor's experiences of brokenness, our connected experiences of brokenness are neither too large nor too small to be honored in the Body. We reach out to one another, addressing the physical, emotional, mental health, family, and individual needs of the whole community and each person within it.

This is hope: This Body will be messy until Christ comes again; it is no less impacted by brokenness than you or I. Even our experience of the Body of Christ will be broken until Christ comes again. But it will never stop being a place where people are connected and belong in a community, even in our seasons of feeling disconnected and disappointed. Instead, we are invited by God into the broken and redeemed Body of Christ to be witnesses of brokenness together—within us and all around us. When Christ comes back for us, we will each be restored, and on that day the community of His Body will also be fully restored. We are each tethered to Christ and His hope. This Body is tethered to Christ and His hope as well. We have a people to belong to.

COMMUNITY

neighbor

1 someone who lives very near to another

2 one who connects with those around them to serve in mercy, to live peaceably, and to share hope

English speakers say *community*. The French say *communauté*. German speakers say *Gemeinschaft*. Modern Greeks call it *koinótita*. Japanese and Arabic speakers each have several distinct words for community in their vernaculars. I especially appreciate that Spanish speakers use *la comunidad* or *la colectividad*, based on the context.

Collected together is more than a nice way to picture community. It reflects accurately how Christians see community of any kind. In Scripture, the people of God are always a transient people. Our home here on earth and all our sociological constructs of community are temporary. In hope, we wait for something more. We wait for an eternal community. Yet we are not left with nothing while we wait. We do wait for the new heaven and new earth that will come when Jesus comes back for us, where community has no connection to poverty, injustice, prejudice, or dissension. We also eagerly anticipate that God has a place in this world for us now. Our places and purposes in communities may shift and change, be transient in this world, but they are not unimportant to God.

Humans like permanence. The transience of this life can be deeply uncomfortable for us—life is always changing, always shifting, and our geographic and local communities are evidence, rather than simply witnesses, of the constant changes. We are tempted to find our identity in what we can see around us— towns, nations, people groups, heritage, among others. Humans tend to lean on shadows of all the good things God gives us in Christ because we can see them; they are in front of our faces today. This is also true for community. Rather than looking to the true community God is crafting for us in His people and in eternity, we grab for identity, community, and a sense of belonging with what's in front of us. The many changes that come into our communities can feel destabilizing, particularly when brokenness makes itself known in our neighborhoods.

It helps to remember that God sees *people* in Christ, not nations or neighborhoods. He upholds *people* in Christ, whether we move or stay put, whether we change or our community changes. God doesn't always intervene to "save" those things we'd like to keep secure, like national borders or school buildings. Psalm 39:5–7 highlights the shortness of our days here and the value of looking forward in Hope to a restored, unchanging community one day even as we live in our ever-changing communities today:

Behold, You have made my days a few handbreadths,
    and my lifetime is as nothing before You.
Surely all mankind stands as a mere breath!
    Surely a man goes about as a shadow!
Surely for nothing they are in turmoil;

man heaps up wealth and does not know who will
gather!

And now, O Lord, for what do I wait?
My hope is in You.

Geographic borders, our heritage and lineage, our collected
interests and clubs, and buildings, new and old, are all fine. They
can be great things to be a part of and to celebrate, but they are
not God. It is important that we recognize these things don't last,
so we do not cling to them. They *feel* more stable to us than they
actually are. Look around at your neighborhood. Consider the
church or school you grew up in. These places are shadows of the
restoration community where we will one day walk and run and
dance with Christ face-to-face. God uses what we know to help
us understand what greater things He is offering us. The roads
we travel every day will crumble. But God's roads in heaven and
in the new creation will stand firm forever. The Father's house is
made of rooms upon rooms where we will live in harmony and
true connectedness and deep knowing forever and ever. We can
also take great hope in the fact that the new creation is both a
place of restoration and a *community* of restoration.

Jesus works to offer restoration in our communities now
while we wait for His community of restoration to come. Now
that you have a name for brokenness, I pray that you help others
name it as well. When you see the hurt and heartache present in
your communities and your heart hurts for your neighbors, I pray
that you connect with them, work together to call brokenness by
name, and help them see hope. Our earthly communities need
hope. When we see brokenness in the places we thought were
stable, it leaves us longing for God and the hope of His restored

community like a deer panting for water, like a lamb seeking the warmth of its Shepherd and its sheepfold.

In Christ, we will one day have a community with no prejudice, no violence, and no crumbling. In that community, the relationships will be perfect and perfectly restored. Until then, finding, creating, and sustaining authentic community will be a whole lot of work. God has a name for this work, a name for the relationships that make up our earthly communities: neighbors. Biblically speaking, you cannot have any kind of community without neighbors.

Loving our neighbor, learning about our neighbor, living alongside our neighbor will take energy. It takes energy to get quality relationships started. It takes energy to keep meaningful relationships going. A community is a larger expression of single relationships. Making community will take more work because there are many relationships. We often picture a community as happenstance or at least organic, not something we have a hand in or any agency over. The truth is that our best relationships, our most authentic relationships, are actually characterized by their effort, not by their mere existence. Christ expends untold effort in keeping relationship with us. While people aren't saved by their effort, God invites us to invest in the relationships all around us. The Gospel goes out as we love our neighbors in a community. Communities grow and deepen when we put effort into building relationships with our neighbors and outwardly extending grace.

We often ask the same questions as the people in the Bible. One person in the New Testament asked, "And who is my neighbor?" Jesus' answer now is the same as it was in Luke 10: The person in the ditch is your neighbor. The one who needs compassion is your neighbor. The broken, the bruised, the one in need—that's your neighbor. (See Luke 10:25–37.)

In the Gospel of Mark (12:28–31), Jesus gives us one simple word for how to care for the neighbors all around us: love. Love God. Love your neighbor. Loving our neighbor is a lot less about good times than it is about that word *sacrifice* again. Loving our neighbor means noticing our neighbor, digging our neighbor out of the ditch of brokenness, bandaging the wounds of brokenness, and bringing them to a place where they can see Hope once again.

We struggle with loving our neighbor because we don't always agree with our neighbor, because our neighbor thinks and acts differently than we do, and because occasionally our neighbor drives us bonkers. And sometimes our neighbors can be unjust, unforgiving, and violent. In *The Book of Forgiving*, Mpho Tutu shares questions so many of us ask when brokenness crashes in through our neighbor's hand: "How did evil get so close to my children? How did I let it get so near?"[22] There are times in brokenness when unthinkable traumas will happen in the communities we thought were so stable, among the neighbors we held so close to our hearts. God's offer of free will extends to all humanity. We are all capable of much good and also much evil. We want peace to prevail in *our* communities. We want them to be different, safer, than what we see happening on the news a world away. But the whole world is broken, and every community along with it. Healing comes only through the hope of Christ. Trauma that remains unhealed, trauma that is given no help and no hope, will beget more trauma.

Even when evil comes so close that we can feel its hot breath, we love our neighbors with words and actions. This love, in the midst of trauma, in the midst of evil, is charged by the hope of

Christ and spreads the hope of Christ. The world is full of assumption and judgment, prejudice and discrimination. We are not better people as Christians; we simply know a better Love. That Love lives in us through the Spirit of the living God. Like the woman in Luke 7:36–50, because we have been forgiven so very much, we are able to love very much. Empathy is our battle cry. Christ's sacrificial love in us is how we bring hope into every community and to every neighbor we encounter.

We are not better people as Christians; we simply know a better Love.

We live with an interesting juxtaposition. We never expect brokenness to get better. We know we carry brokenness within us and will see it all around us until Jesus comes back again. But that doesn't mean we do not or should not fight against injustice, against violence, against all the things that create fear and hurt in our communities. We know that Jesus can and will work in us and through us to love our neighbor, to share His hope with a broken world, to impact our communities with positive change.

This is hope: We are not hopeless until Jesus comes again. We hold His hope in us because He is coming again. His love going out does make the world a better place. In our short time on earth, God gives us communities to live in and people to connect with. God is not limited by geography and does not limit us by geography or club membership or other collective investments. God invites us to be part of something bigger. We exist in our given spaces and places as somebody's neighbor. When we share Christ's love and hope with our neighbor during our time here, we make an eternal impact. When we see injustice, we can fight it. When we see violence and hurt, poverty and privilege, we respond with the hope He has put inside of us.

MESSES IN CREATION:
A BROKEN WORLD

name

1 to give identity and thereby recognition to something or someone

2 to specify in order to make something identifiable or known

My in-laws live on a quiet street with Lake Huron spread out beyond their front yard. My husband and I like to put our kayaks in
during the early morning hours, when the birds are just starting
to move and the city still lies sleeping. If you paddle out past
the docks to where the city park is just a blur, it's like another world—just you, the water, and God. I like to set my paddle
across my legs and meet with Him there, to ponder all the things
around me that He created. I like to ask Him the questions that
have been stored up in my chest for far too long. The words of
Psalm 121 come easily to mind during these times, some verses
sticking better than others in my memory:

> I lift up my eyes to the hills.
> From where does my help come?
> My help comes from the LORD,

who made heaven and earth. . . .
Behold, He who keeps Israel
will neither slumber nor sleep. . . .
The LORD will keep
your going out and your coming in
from this time forth and forevermore. (vv. 1–2, 4, 8)

We all need some time in a real or metaphorical kayak—a chance to experience a unique quiet in the tumultuousness of life. I remember being a young adult and thinking most moments of life were like those in my kayak—serene and full of promise. As I grew older, life's storms pummeled, and I became acutely aware that serenity and promise are nice, but they are not all there is to God's plans and purposes.

Every time I take my kayak out on those glass-water mornings, I sit a moment longer and dread putting my paddle back into the water of Lake Huron. With no one else and nothing else around to disturb the water, it is only my paddle that breaks the quiet, my fault that the peace is broken. When I watch my paddle enter the perfect water, I feel like I am breaking something beautiful. But I also don't know how to stop it. I need to get back to the house and take care of my children. I need to clean up our breakfast messes and continue with our plans for the day.

I shatter the glass water, and it reminds me of life's imperfection. There is a weight to that imperfection. We can sense it and see it, but we very often don't know what to call it. We look around us at the world and feel so very helpless. Sometimes we can own that shattering; we clearly see our broken actions, our part in the brokenness, the hurts we have caused. We can name our sin and confess it. There, we find healing in Christ.

Other times in life, we call out someone else and their paddle. When other people's sin creates waves of unrest and destruction in our lives, it's important to call it by name—truth in love, love in truth. Healing comes here through Christ, in forgiveness and sometimes also in new boundaries.

What is harder to understand are the murky things of brokenness, the rippling in the water everywhere when we can't see the paddles causing it. Some brokenness doesn't have a clear source beyond that blasted fruit on a tree, and even less clear solutions in our daily lives. Nothing is untouched by sin; nothing is untouched by that fruit. When the fruit fell from Eve's and Adam's hands onto the ground, it left ripples. You hold that sin. I hold that sin. Our neighbors hold that sin. The world itself holds that sin. We are not responsible for *all* brokenness. Even though our paddles didn't create every ripple in the water, we still see them, know them, live with them. We will always sense the weight of brokenness because we share in a life that's bigger than us, connections that are more than what we can see in front of our faces.

The ripples of sin in the waters of this world are weighty. According to Romans 8:22–23, the whole earth groans in the pains of the brokenness in this world: "For we know that the whole creation has been groaning together in the pains of childbirth until now. And not only the creation, but we ourselves, who have the firstfruits of the Spirit, groan inwardly as we wait eagerly for adoption as sons, the redemption of our bodies." We can see these groans in the earthquakes and the famines, the locusts and the floods. We hear the atmosphere groan under its ozone hole and the icebergs crack in fluctuating temperatures.

Calling the brokenness of the world what it is, knowing it's not just me, but the whole universe that holds brokenness inside of it—that takes the weight off of my shoulders. Yes, we are broken people. We are born sinful and broken from birth, disintegrated and hurting, helpless without God. We will groan in that pain until He comes. But groaning isn't our whole story.

If "we are broken people" and "I'm broken" are our only understandings of this concept we call brokenness and the state of the world we see around us, the shame is overwhelming. This shame is the devil's shovel as he tries to bury us in a pit of brokenness. Just as we cannot dig ourselves or our neighbors out of our sin-filled pits, we can't dig the world out of its pit of brokenness either. We easily turn these things inward and carry the shame of brokenness around with us into our families, our workplaces, and our communities. God hears our groaning. Jesus surely can dig us out and surely does dig us out. While we all bear our sufferings and struggles, the shame of brokenness was borne by Christ on the cross long ago; we do not have to carry it around with us. In Christ and through His Word, God gives us eyes to see, ears to hear, and minds to know in order to call the devil's games by name.

The only one who can do anything to save the whole universe is Jesus. Jesus didn't deserve the weight of all the brokenness, but He is where the weight of brokenness belongs because He can handle it. He has handled it. Jesus *can* solve the problem of brokenness. Jesus *has* solved the problem of brokenness. Jesus *continues* to solve the problem of brokenness. The cross gives us much-needed forgiveness for our personal brokenness and renews our ability to connect with God in relationship despite our universal brokenness.

In Romans 8:31–35, the writer, Paul, asks rhetorical questions. He knows the answer, just as all of us in Christ know the answer.

But he asks anyway, for his own benefit and for ours. It is easy to forget we don't have to hold the shame of brokenness in ourselves. It is easy to forget that we are not alone in the brokenness all around us in this world. The answer to each of Paul's questions below is *nothing*. Not even brokenness.

> What then shall we say to these things? If God is for
> us, who can be against us? He who did not spare His
> own Son but gave Him up for us all, how will He not
> also with Him graciously give us all things? Who shall
> bring any charge against God's elect? It is God who
> justifies. Who is to condemn? Christ Jesus is the one
> who died—more than that, who was raised—who is
> at the right hand of God, who indeed is interceding
> for us. Who shall separate us from the love of Christ?
> Shall tribulation, or distress, or persecution, or famine,
> or nakedness, or danger, or sword?

The devil uses brokenness to separate. He tries to use our struggles and the struggles of this world to drive a wedge of hopelessness between us and God. He also tries to use brokenness as a wedge in all our relationships between one another. Satan thinks broken identity can steal our hope. He thinks broken connection can rob our hope. He thinks broken community can tear away our hope. Brokenness could have separated us from hope, but God said, "No." Jesus Christ is God's every "Yes" to us in the middle of all the brokenness (2 Corinthians 1:20).

Jesus Christ is God's every "Yes" to us in the middle of all the brokenness.

The Holy Spirit, using Paul's pen, gave us the beginning of a list of all the broken things of this world the devil would use to try to separate us from the hope we have in Christ. Here is a list of just a few manifestations of the brokenness we carry in this life from my own pen. These are the ones I hear about most often, in no particular order:

- death, and the sense of loss and grief that go with it
- trauma—big, little, medium, invisible, individual, collective
- suicide and the holes it leaves behind
- heartbreak—romantic, friendship, family, global
- mental illness and mental health struggles
- mental health stigma
- sexual and gender identity struggles
- war and rumors of war
- natural disasters—fear, destruction, loss, the aftermath
- abortion
- abuse and neglect—children, elderly, and every age in between
- racism
- trying to make it out of junior high and high school with some sense of identity and purpose
- wanting children, wanting more children
- wondering if our children still love us
- the angst that comes with change, even if it grows us

- pressure to succeed (whatever that means)
- lack—I'm not enough, we don't have enough, nothing will ever be enough
- betrayal and broken trust—in marriage, in friendship, in vocation, in the Church
- physical illness
- loneliness
- questions of worth

My list is far from all-inclusive. When I started writing this book, I wanted to name not just these few, but all the broken things. I wanted it to be a place to address and to honor every one of your broken hurts and broken hardships. But as I wrote, new kinds of brokenness kept rising to the surface, demanding attention. I began to realize that there is not enough space on the page or enough pages in the world to address all the brokenness. But I pray this book helps you call your own experiences of brokenness by name. I pray it helps you name brokenness in the world when you see it in your neighborhood and on the news. I pray that with this book you now have the ability to sit across from a friend or your child and help call those hard and heavy experiences what they are—brokenness. But not brokenness only. Brokenness touched by Hope.

CONCLUSION

TURNING TOWARD HOPE

restoration

1 returning something to its owner in its original condition

2 the time when Jesus will come again from the heavens to stand on the earth and return the universe to its original condition without sin, without tears, without hurt

3 when all things will be made new in the fullness of life in Christ Jesus

We do not walk through this life in brokenness only; we walk in brokenness touched by Hope. Sometimes it's so hard to see. And sometimes we spend so much time trying to avoid the brokenness that it's actually harder to see Hope. Hope is seen through the brokenness, not in spite of it. When we name the brokenness, we are really turning toward Hope.

Our broken things are never left untouched by God. The cross was brokenness, foolishness to humans, but to God it was the way to save the whole world (1 Corinthians 1:18–25). The world may be groaning, our family and friends may be groaning, our communities may groan, the Body of Christ may groan, but Hope groans with us. And Hope is louder. Romans 8:26–27 promises us that the Holy Spirit will match every groan, even those for which we have no words:

> Likewise the Spirit helps us in our weakness. For we do not know what to pray for as we ought, but the Spirit Himself intercedes for us with groanings too deep for words. And He who searches hearts knows what is the mind of the Spirit, because the Spirit intercedes for the saints according to the will of God.

When we have no words, we can still call our struggle by name: brokenness.

The Spirit turns us toward hope for today and the bright hope of the future. God is with us. God sits alongside us. God is with our families, our friendships, our communities. Jesus *is* coming back for us. He will not leave us here in this mess and shattered existence. Even if the good parts of life have always outweighed the challenging parts for you, the reality of brokenness is everywhere. But the reality of brokenness will not always be our reality.

Can you imagine the comfort of Jesus, but in a bolder and brighter version, without all the hindrances of brokenness pressing against us?

There is a different life in the new creation to come. It will feel gently familiar and breathtakingly new all at the same time. Can you imagine the comfort of Jesus, but in a bolder and brighter version, without all the hindrances of brokenness pressing against us? Revelation gives us the best vantage point of what that restoration will look like and feel like. The Bible only gives us abstract imagery and language wrapped in metaphor when it speaks of the new creation, but the picture it presents of these brighter days is blazing with hope:

> I saw a new heaven and a new earth, for the first heaven and the first earth had passed away, and the sea was no more. And I saw the holy city, new Jerusalem, coming down out of heaven from God, prepared as a bride adorned for her husband. And I heard a loud voice from the throne saying, "Behold, the dwelling place of God is with man. He will dwell with them, and they will be His people, and God Himself will be with them as their God. He will wipe away every tear from their eyes, and death shall be no more, neither shall there be mourning, nor crying, nor pain anymore, for the former things have passed away." (Revelation 21:1–4)

I was once in a mental health class where the instructor shared this acronym:[23]

Hold
On
Pain
Ends

The previous things will pass away. The pain of the previous things will not always be there. The joy of the previous things cannot compare to what is to come for us in Christ.

We each want to know that brokenness ends. We want the world to be a better place for us, for our children, for future generations, and for our friends, but everything we do feels like only a drop in the bucket. Turn toward hope. Hope reminds us that this life and all its brokenness isn't all there is for us. God is faithful. He gives us strength for this day to bring more hope into the world. God's hope poured out of us into our time and place makes the world a better place. We fight the good fight in hope. We care for the weary in hope. When we are a voice for the voiceless, we shout hope into this world.

People may not seem hungry for Jesus, but they *are* hungry for the difference faith makes.

In all the brokenness, sometimes we lose sight of the truth: The pain will end. Jesus is real. He is here with us now, and He is coming soon. People may not seem hungry for Jesus, but they *are* hungry for the difference faith makes. We help them turn toward Hope by being willing to help them name their brokenness. They want to know the reality of a new beginning, without the same old ending of broken every time. We bring hope into this world by sitting with them and helping them name the gnawing in their stomach. We help them call the disappointment of brokenness by name and give them space to ask questions and wrestle with the One who is the daily bread for our hunger. We acknowledge the source of our hope and call Him by name as we share our story of hope.

I know sometimes hope is hard to see and seems very far off in our own lives. I don't know about you, but I am impatient. I want Jesus to solve brokenness now, or yesterday, or last Sunday. Praise God He does not judge me by my patience nor operate by my clock. Christ is patient when I am not. People matter so much to Him. He waits and waits and waits for people to be told of Him and for people to turn to Him, because He loves each and every one of us. He loves us when we fail to notice Him. He loves us when we refuse to recognize Him as Savior, as Friend, as Freedom. He loves us when we feel we have no hope in Him.

Romans 8:24–25 gives us an anchor when we need reminders amid the brokenness to keep turning toward hope. Hold tight to these verses: "For in this hope we were saved. Now hope that is seen is not hope. For who hopes for what he sees? But if we hope for what we do not see, we wait for it with patience." When we cannot see hope, the Bible offers it to us on each page. There are 164 appearances of the word *hope* in the ESV translation of Scripture, 180 in the NIV, and 190 in the NLT. I need that amount of hope in the brokenness of every day.

While ice skating on a small frozen pond in Minnesota last winter, I was struck by how many cracks there were in the ice. I asked the woman manning the warming hut if it was safe to skate on the ice with so many cracks. She looked at me with compassion and said, "Oh sweetie, there are several good inches of ice under those cracks."

Christ is the good ice underneath all our cracks. Christ is the firm foundation upon which we skate and walk and crawl and eat and sleep in this life. As Christians, we have a name for our hope and also a name for the hurtful, challenging, frustrating, and weighty things of this life. When we call brokenness out by naming the scary cracks in our lives, we can see the foundation beyond those cracks a little more clearly. First Peter 5:10 holds a promise of that firm, crystal-clear foundation: "And after you have suffered a little while, the God of all grace, who has called you to His eternal glory in Christ, will Himself restore, confirm, strengthen, and establish you."

This is hope: God is restoring, confirming, strengthening, and establishing us in Christ *every day*. Jesus picks us up and places us on His solid foundation again and again and again. When we help one another look at all the cracks on this big lake of life, we give all the messes a place to be called what they are: broken . . . but with hope.

God integrates. God restores—in pieces now and in completeness one day. God brings wholeness and hope in His time and in His ways for each of us. God enters into this mess. Sometimes we see Him cleaning up and clearing away the messes in our lives. More often, He lets hope shine in the middle of the brokenness, using it for purposes, connections, and integrations we may or may not see.

We live in His hope. We wait in His hope, and we hand off His hope. We rest in His hope when we are sad, when life is confusing and hard. We watch for His hope. Sometimes we might need to head back to therapy to help us name the burdens on our chest and remember the hope in our lungs. We pray for His hope to invade our families, our friendships, our churches, and our communities. We absorb hope from our Bibles.

Jesus is that hope. In all the brokenness, Jesus is living hope.

Jesus turns our hearts, our minds, and our spirits toward Himself each day. We wait for the day when this whole world will see just who He is, bright and blazing with hope. In the meantime, we call brokenness out of its corner and call it by name. We turn toward God when the brokenness presses in and makes us want to turn away. In the power of Christ, we pray and we seek and we connect and we continue on, because God has made a way. In the middle of our brokenness, God brings restoration. This is where we find hope.

READER GUIDE

Preface: What Is Brokenness?

How would you define *brokenness* in your own words?

Do you think people are resistant to the idea of brokenness? Why or why not?

Introduction: From Brokenness to Hope

Where and how do you see the impact of brokenness on you as an individual?

Where do you see brokenness all around you?

In what ways do you see people today communicating—whether they realize it or not—that they need hope?

Messes in Me: Broken Identity

BROKENNESS AND DISINTEGRATION

Where is disintegration evident when you look around yourself?

Considering that God knits our inward beings together, according to Psalm 139, what systems or workings inside you are miraculous when you stop and think about it?

Where have you seen God reintegrate something in your life?

BODY IMAGE

Which element of self is hardest for you to value—body, heart, mind, or soul? Why?

Considering 1 Corinthians 15:42–43, how would you describe the brokenness of our bodies and souls? How would you describe the resurrection we have alive in our bodies and souls in Christ?

How do we love the body God created, care for it, and yet not worship it or demean it?

EMOTION

What are some of the most complex emotions you have experienced in life?

How do you most often deal with your emotions? What does it look like when you give your emotions space as informants but not leaders in your life?

How does God, the Creator of emotions, help us be informed by our emotions but not led by them?

RESILIENCE

What images come to mind when you read the definition of *resilience*? What best represents hard-won resilience to you?

What traumas and life challenges do you see people facing in the Bible?

How has God built resilience in you?

VULNERABILITY

What things made you feel vulnerable as a child? What things remind you that you are still vulnerable as an adult?

What characteristics and actions of God help you feel comforted in your vulnerability before God?

How does brokenness impact our vulnerability with other people? How does restoration impact our vulnerability with other people?

Messes in Family: Broken Intimacy

SAFETY AND KNOWING

What kinds of experiences in family life impact our sense of safety in this world?

Every family has their own story of brokenness in the world and in their own homes. In what ways have you seen God restore intimacy, safety, and knowing in family life?

CHILDHOOD

In what ways is it complicated to know that God names all families and placed us in our families? In what ways is it comforting?

What was your family of origin like? Where was brokenness evident in your family of origin? Where was God's grace evident for you in your childhood?

Where have you found family in other places beyond your biological family of origin?

ROMANTIC RELATIONSHIPS

In what ways do you find relationships to be a lot of work? Which relationships in your life are especially a lot of work for you and why?

In what ways do we treat marriage or being single as superior options against each other rather than different places to be in life? How might we support one another better in our life choices regarding romantic relationships?

How might we better support the marriages around us?

FAMILY LIFE

What is the picture in your head of "normal" family life? How does the phrase "broken is normal" transform that picture?

In what ways do families and the Body of Christ complement each other? How might you find them competing against each other in a broken world?

How does God's love and honor for us and God's love and honor in us change the way we interact in our families?

Messes in Community: Broken Belonging

CONNECTION AND BELONGING

In what ways does brokenness contribute to disconnection with God, with people, with the world as a whole?

How does our sense of identity but also *belonging* in Christ change the way we interact with people in our lives?

Which layer(s) of loneliness—emotional, social, collective—have you struggled with before, or which one do you struggle with most right now?

FRIENDSHIP

Which is more challenging for you: beginning a friendship or continuing a friendship? Why?

What makes bidding or abiding with someone intimidating?

Why are we often afraid of awkwardness in relationships? What are some of the awkward moments you have had when forging friendships or deepening friendships?

What is the difference between a friendship and being a part of the same Body of Christ?

THE BODY OF CHRIST

In what areas do you see the Body of Christ impacted by brokenness the most? Share some examples.

How do the bonds of the Body of Christ and our belonging within the Body of Christ equip us and send us out into the world?

In what practical ways can we support people to be individuals in the Body of Christ and also see themselves as a unified whole within the Body of Christ?

COMMUNITY

Consider your communities. What are the commonalities that hold these communities together? What shadow of the comforts of Christ do you find in these communities?

In what ways does knowing we are transient in Christ here on this earth change our perspective of our communities?

After reading the biblical and practical insight in this chapter, how would you define who your neighbor is and what that relationship looks like, even while we live in brokenness?

What gets in our way of being empathetic to our neighbors?

Messes in Creation: A Broken World

What power and healing is there in calling brokenness by name with the hope of Christ in you?

How do you see brokenness and hope differently now than when you first began reading this book?

What broken things of life would you add to the list from this section?

Conclusion: Turning toward Hope

What are you most looking forward to in the restoration of all things when Christ Jesus comes again?

ENDNOTES

1   Jeffrey A. Gibbs, *Matthew 21:1–28:20*, Concordia Commentary (St. Louis: Concordia Publishing House, 2018), 1150.

2   EMDRIA, "Trauma and the Brain: EMDR Therapy Can Help," https://mk0emdrias990sg9utnb.kinstacdn.com/wp-content /uploads/2020/04/final_trauma_and_the_brain.pdf. Accessed June 26, 2020.

3   See Fulvio D'Acquisto, "Affective Immunology: Where Emotions and the Immune Response Converge," *Psychoneuroimmunology Dialogues in Clinical Neuroscience* 19, no. 1 (2017): 9–19, https:// www.ncbi.nlm.nih.gov/pmc/articles/PMC5442367/; and Viktoriya Maydych, "The Interplay between Stress, Inflammation, and Emotional Attention: Relevance for Depression," *Frontiers in Neuroscience* 13 (2019): 384, https://www.ncbi.nlm.nih.gov/pmc /articles/PMC6491771/.

4   See Ja Y. Lee, Kristen A. Lindquist, and Chang S. Nam, "Emotion- al Granularity Effects on Event-Related Brain Potentials during Affective Picture Processing," *Frontiers in Human Neuroscience* (March 24, 2017), https://www.frontiersin.org/articles/10.3389 /fnhum.2017.00133/full; and Lisa Feldman Barrett, *How Emotions Are Made: The Secret Life of the Brain* (Boston: Houghton Mifflin Harcourt, 2017).

5   Devika Duggal, Amanda Sacks-Zimmerman, and Taylor Liberta, "The Impact of Hope and Resilience on Multiple Factors in Neurosurgical Patients," *Cureus* (October 26, 2016), https://www.ncbi.nlm.nih.gov/pmc/articles/PMC5120968/.

6   Brené Brown, *Daring Greatly* (New York: Avery Penguin Random House, 2012), 34.

7   Andy Bates, David Fleming, and Heidi Goehmann, "Faith'n'Family—Should I Talk to a Pastor or Psychologist?" KFUO Radio, December 20, 2017, https://www.kfuo.org/2017/12/20/faf-122017-pastor-psychologist/. Accessed May 17, 2020.

8   Strong's Hebrew: 3045. yada—to know, accessed June 26, 2020, https://biblehub.com/hebrew/3045.htm.

9   Anna R. Brandon et al., "A History of the Theory of Prenatal Attachment," *Journal of Prenatal and Perinatal Psychology and Health* (U.S. National Library of Medicine, 2009), https://www.ncbi.nlm.nih.gov/pmc/articles/PMC3083029/.

10 Amir Levine and Rachel Heller, *Attached: The New Science of Adult Attachment and How It Can Help You Find—and Keep—Love* (New York: Penguin, 2011).

11 Francine Shapiro, *Getting Past Your Past: Take Control of Your Life with Self-Help Techniques from EMDR Therapy* (Emmaus, PA: Rodale, 2014), 89.

12 For more on this confusing scriptural tidbit, see my Bible study on the Song of Songs, *Altogether Beautiful* (St. Louis: Concordia Publishing House, 2018).

13 Greek Concordance: mega—18 occurrences, accessed June 29, 2020, https://biblehub.com/greek/mega_3173.htm.

14 Strong's Greek: 5563. chórizó—to separate, divide, accessed June 29, 2020, https://biblehub.com/greek/5563.htm.

15 John Mordechai Gottman and Nan Silver, *The Seven Principles for Making Marriage Work: A Practical Guide from the Country's Foremost Relationship Expert* (New York: Harmony Books, 2015), 87–90.

16 Sihyun Park and Kyung Sook Park, "Family Stigma: A Concept Analysis," *Asian Nursing Research* 8, no. 3 (2014): 165–71, https://doi.org/10.1016/j.anr.2014.02.006.

17 Terry Clark-Jones, "Qualities of a Healthy Family," MSU Extension, April 2, 2018, https://www.canr.msu.edu/news/traits_of_a_healthy_family.

18 Vivek Hallegere Murthy, *Together: The Healing Power of Human Connection in a Sometimes Lonely World* (New York: HarperCollins, 2020), 8. © 2020 by Vivek Murthy. Used by permission of HarperCollins Publishers.

19 "The Health Benefits of Good Friends," Mayo Clinic (Mayo Foundation for Medical Education and Research, August 24, 2019), https://www.mayoclinic.org/healthy-lifestyle/adult-health/in-depth/friendships/art-20044860.

20 C. S. Lewis, *The Four Loves* (San Francisco: HarperOne, 2017), 83. © CS Lewis Pte Ltd 1960. Used with permission.

21 John Mordechai Gottman and Joan DeClaire, *The Relationship Cure: A Five-Step Guide to Strengthening Your Marriage, Family, and Friendships* (New York: Harmony Books, 2002), 4.

22 Desmond M. Tutu and Mpho A. Tutu, *The Book of Forgiving: The Fourfold Path for Healing Ourselves and Our World*, ed. Douglas Carlton Abrams (London: William Collins, 2015), 107. © 2014 by Desmond M. Tutu and Mpho A. Tutu. Used by permission of HarperCollins.

23 Samuel Kee, *Soul Tattoo: A Life and Spirit Bearing the Marks of God* (Colorado Springs: David C Cook, 2014), 90–91. © 2014 by Samuel Kee. Used by permission of David C Cook. May not be further reproduced. All rights reserved.

ACKNOWLEDGMENTS

To Sarah, Barbara, Katie, Josh and Sarah, and Dave for helping me get my messy thoughts onto paper and helping me call the brokenness by name more clearly;

To Jamie, Laura, Holli, Elizabeth, the design team, and the whole CPH team—thank you! These books would never become books without you all;

To Macee, Jonah, Jyeva, and Zeke for listening without fail every time I wanted to talk about brokenness again;

To my sisters for helping me remember that my broken words mattered;

To my clients who continuously inspire me to speak truth to trauma, do the hard work of showing up, and believe in restoration, even when it looks like the broken pieces will never fit back together;

To Jesus, Anchor, Foundation, Help, and Life. You are our only Hope.